RUNNING: CHEAPER THAN THERAPY

RUNNING:

CHEAPER

A CELEBRATION
OF RUNNING

THAN

THERAPY

Chas Newkey-Burden

B L O O M S B U R Y

LONDON · OXFORD · NEW YORK · NEW DELHI · SYDNEY

Bloomsbury Sport
An imprint of Bloomsbury Publishing Plc

50 Bedford Square
London
WC1B 3DP
UK

1385 Broadway
New York
NY 10018
USA

www.bloomsbury.com

BLOOMSBURY and the Diana logo are trademarks of
Bloomsbury Publishing Plc

First published 2017
© Chas Newkey-Burden, 2017
Illustrations by Ana Roa Szwarcberg, aroastock.com

Chas Newkey-Burden has asserted his right under the Copyright, Designs and
Patents Act, 1988, to be identified as the Author of this work.

All suggestions and material in this book are for information purposes only.
Since each individual's personal situation, health history and lifestyle differs
you should use discretion before proceeding to do any of the exercises or
techniques described. The author and publisher expressly disclaim any
responsibility for any adverse reactions or effects that may result from
the use or interpretation of the information contained within this book.

British Library Cataloguing-in-Publication Data
A catalogue record for this book is available from the British Library.

Library of Congress Cataloguing-in-Publication data has been applied for.

ISBN: Print: 978-1-4729-4883-0
ePDF: 978-1-4729-4882-3
ePub: 978-1-4729-4880-9

8 10 9 7

Typeset in Chaparral Pro by Deanta Global Publishing Service, Chennai, India
Printed and bound in Great Britain by CPI Group (UK) Ltd. Croydon, CR0 4YY

MIX
Paper from
responsible sources
FSC® C013604

To find out more about our authors and books visit www.bloomsbury.com.
Here you will find extracts, author interviews, details of forthcoming events
and the option to sign up for our newsletters

Introduction

Try and name an activity that *always* makes you feel better.

Tricky, isn't it? Even indulgent treats such as shopping, drinking or holidays can leave you feeling a bit unmoved or unfulfilled, especially afterwards. And the earth can't always move between the sheets.

For many of us, when we want a guaranteed lift, little can compete with running – it is so unanswerably genuine and so democratically approachable. It just always rewards you, doesn't it?

From a short jog around the park that nudges your mood gently upwards to longer outings that produce a lengthy buzz or the closing stages of the marathon when you feel physically demolished but emotionally invincible all at once, it delivers every time.

If someone could bottle what running gives you, they would make a fortune. But they cannot, so we must put on our trainers and get out there to find it.

A compendium of wisdom and humour, the pages ahead try to do justice to that search. In them, we take a look at the familiar archetypes of the running community, from the nutrition nut and unsolicited coach to the gadget guru and the inexplicably good old dear.

We also examine everything from jogging etiquette to the 26.2 things that always happen when you tackle a marathon, and the connection between running and smoking cannabis. There

are also stats, tips and anecdotes, the funniest signs ever seen at marathons, and so much more.

Guest contributors including Olympic medallist Liz Yelling, political strategist Alastair Campbell and comedian David Baddiel all trot by to offer their thoughts, whereas others explain how running helped them beat cancer, get over a violent attack or write a best-selling novel.

As a collection of musings, the book is intentionally as varied and random as the entrants you see at any running event: from the solemn science that leads the charge to the middle ground that takes it all kind of seriously, but not too seriously, and then the more light-hearted stragglers at the back, who can see how daft a lot of the running experience is but love it all the more for that.

Running is, ultimately, both daft and divine. In these crazy times, if you want to feel a bit better about the world, there's no more dependable friend than a dash in the great outdoors.

And it's cheaper than therapy...

Chas Newkey Burden, 2017.

26 Reasons to Run

1. Happiness

We want to set off for this motivational marathon in the best of spirits, so let's start with a particularly happy fact: numerous studies have shown that running reduces stress, anxiety and depression. It helps to make you feel better in both the short and long term.

In fact, according to a recent study, the 'runner's high' is aptly named: we feel jubilation after a long period of exertion due to a rush of chemical substances called cannabinoids, the same stuff that's found in marijuana. A healthier high!

2. Immune boost

Running for up to an hour at a moderate intensity bolsters your immune system, by accelerating the circulation of protective cells.

3. Stronger knees

Lazy people will tell you that running is bad for your knees. Well, wave this fact in their face: according to Boston University, regular running actually improves knee health. It also strengthens bones and joints.

4. It's cheap!

Gym memberships drain your bank account, particularly once you include the joining fee, padlock charge and all those other sneaky little add-ons. Bikes are expensive to buy and maintain. Swimming costs you every time you do it. Running, however, is the cheapest of exercise regimes. The only significant cost is a new pair of running shoes every 800 kilometres (500 miles) or so.

5. A longer life

Jogging can extend your time on the planet. Studies show that exercising helps you to live longer by as much as 5.3 years.

6. Discovery

Jog around your neighbourhood regularly and you begin to discover local wonders you never knew existed. As you stumble upon hidden parks, secret riverbanks and other esoteric delights, you'll feel like an heroic explorer.

7. Humility

Many beginners assume that they'll be universally laughed and pointed at as they run down the street in their shorts but, as they quickly discover, nobody pays much attention to what they're doing. This is a useful reality check for life.

8. Core blimey!

You may not instinctively link running with the strengthening of the core, but it actually gives these muscles a workout thanks to the spinal rotation involved. If your regular route includes uneven surfaces, all the rebalancing involved will only enhance this.

9. A younger mind

We create fewer brain cells as we get older. However, scientists at the University of Cambridge led by behavioural neuroscientist Timothy Bussey said in 2010 that regular running reverses this development, keeping your mind young.

10. Lower cancer risk

A colossal study in the *Journal of Nutrition* linked regular exercise with a lower risk of some cancers. Also, according to research by *Runner's World*, for those with cancer, sensible running can enhance their quality of life while they're undergoing chemotherapy.

11. Greater memory

OK, we're into double figures, so remember this: running boosts the production of neurotrophic factors. These chemicals, which stimulate brain growth, focus especially on the wonderfully named hippocampus region, the place where your memories are stored. Get out there and run your way to elephantine recall.

12. Lower blood pressure

A report from the American Heart Association published in 2013 in the (wonderfully monikered) journal *Hypertension* found that men and women at all blood-pressure levels benefit from regular running and other aerobic activity, including those with hypertension. Just 30–40 minutes of jogging several days a week can help prevent or reduce hypertension.

13. Dat ass!

To celebrate reaching the halfway point, here's a cheeky fact for you: running activates your glutes, making it one of the fastest and most painless routes to a lifted and more toned butt. (Do stop pretending you don't want one.)

14. Moving scenery

Working out in the gym can be like starring in the most boring movie ever made. The sweaty, grimacing weightlifter. The woman glued to the cross-trainer. The televisions permanently tuned to depressing, rolling news channels. Well, outdoor running offers a gripping, rolling nature documentary of imagery to keep your enthusiasm flowing.

15. Healthier heart

Want to improve your circulation and reduce the risk of a heart attack, high blood pressure and strokes? Running for just an hour each week can lower the risk of heart disease by almost 50 per cent.

16. Everyday advantage

As you go about your daily business you will be thankful to be a runner. Late for a train? Catch it without losing your breath. Ascending a steep staircase with colleagues? Smile magnanimously as you reach the top before everyone else. Playing with your kids in the park? Show up the wheezing parents around you.

17. Sweeter dreams

Studies show that runners find it easier to get to sleep at night and sleep for longer.

18. A clearer complexion

Jogging can improve your complexion by enhancing the transportation of nutrients around your system and flushing out waste products. This will help make your skin clearer and give you that distinctive runner's glow.

19. More confidence

Of all forms of exercise, running is arguably the fastest route to greater confidence. In a study, those who ran in the open air showed higher levels of post-workout self-esteem than those who huffed away inside a gym.

20. Community spirit

You'll need a boost as you head into the 20s. And whether you grab a jogging buddy, join your neighbourhood running club or head down to your local parkrun, running can be a pathway to a new network of friends.

21. More 'me time'

Or, if you are craving some time alone, what better pastime than running? Leave your phone at home and head out into the great outdoors. In the 21st century it is a rare treat to be un-contactable for any length of time. Bask in the anonymity and freedom!

22. Do it anywhere

Run near where you live, run near where you work, run on holiday, run on mountains, run by the beach, run down the high street. You won't find another fitness hobby that can be practised so universally.

23. Guilt-free eating

Want to have another scoop of pasta, or a slice of cake? Just add a few miles to your next run, and tuck in, free of calorific guilt.

24. Save money

If you are looking for a new ready-made excuse to avoid expensive pub sessions, costly visits to restaurants and other finance-draining activities, then take up running!

25. Boost concentration

Are you still with us? If you're a runner, the answer should be 'yes'. Research carried out at Rhode Island College found that running boosts creativity and concentration by increasing brain activity for up to two hours after a workout.

26. Between the sheets

Running is an excellent form of cardiovascular exercise, which means it boosts your endurance, and sexual performance is heightened by greater endurance levels. And if that fact doesn't keep you going, nothing will.

Funny Spectator Signs at Running Events

Runners You Know: The nutrition nut

For these runners, the athletic experience takes place as much in their kitchen as it does in the local park or on the running track.

Everything that passes through these runners' mouths is carefully measured. Their skinny fingers scoop wartime-ration portions of rice into the kitchen scales before cooking. As they get home after a run they carefully assemble shakes packed with obscure fruits, oils, powders and other potions, and swallow them down their pencil-thin necks.

They always boil, rather than fry, chicken and fish. Baffling mathematics determines how many carbs they are permitted at each sitting, depending on whether it's a high-intensity, moderate or easy running day. They are always ahead of the curve on every foodie fad.

The nutrition nut eternally grasps a bottle of filtered water, because hydration is so important, don't you know. They turn up their noses at alcohol, chocolate and other calorific mischief-makers, but they've got broccoli and bananas sprouting out of their ears.

You can spot them during a run. They will be the ones carrying beetroot (beet) shots, or systematically sipping water rather than necking huge gulps every few miles like the rest of the pack. Approach them at any stage in a race and they will be only too happy to tell you their exact glycogen levels.

In their quest for the best way to take in extra micronutrients they regularly haunt the aisles of their local health-food store – skinny, spectral figures, like something from a war documentary.

They wouldn't be top of many lists as dinner party hosts, but all this judicious consumption does help make the nutrition nut a very effective runner.

Did you Know?

Research at Newcastle University found that men aged 55 to 65 who ran more than 64 kilometres (40 miles) a week had higher levels of testosterone and growth hormone than their sedentary equivalents.

Remember...

Cross-training helps you avoid injury.

Running Wisdom

In 2015, the *Journal of Psychiatric Research* published the results of a 12-week study that concluded that exercise is beneficial for those suffering from post-traumatic stress disorder (PTSD). Taking a standard 12-week care programme for those suffering from the condition, it compared the results of the programme when exercise was added into the mix. The results showed that the injection of exercise led to further reductions in PTSD, depression and sleep disruption.

Running Philosophy

❝ We are designed to run and we increase our chance of daily happiness **❞** when we do so.

Jeff Galloway, running coach

Funny Spectator Signs at Running Events

My Running Story:
Comedian and Author Mark Watson

Last year I did my first Great North Run in North-east England.
I hadn't quite realised the sheer size of the event, which is
somewhat naive given the fact that it publicises itself as 'the
world's biggest half marathon' and the same slogan is yelled at you
every two minutes as you approach the start line.

Among the many runners I chatted to during the long wait to
get going was a team all done out in the blue vests of an athletics
club. They were checking watches and chewing their final gel pads
and talking about PBs and 'the conditions'. There's little more
intimidating at the start of a long race than a big group of people
who look like they really know what they're doing.

About two-thirds into the race I sailed past this whole group,
most of whom were visibly suffering in the unexpected sunshine.
Their bluster was gone: a couple of them were barely moving. It's
poor form to take strength from the struggles of others – in a
race and in the world more generally – but there's no denying it
gave me an extra boost. I came into the final mile feeling I had
plenty, as they say, in the tank. Down the final straight, along
South Shields beach, I was conscious of a lot of people cheering
and shouting in my direction. Had they recognised the guy from
2008/9-era *Mock The Week*? I felt adrenalin swilling through me
just in time for the final push. About 100 metres (100 yards) from
home, a man in a full-body Scooby Doo costume – the one they
HAD been cheering for – breezed past me and broke the tape,
having outrun me over 13.1 miles dressed as a cartoon dog.

Running teaches us a lot of life lessons. The people who project
the greatest confidence are often just concealing insecurities.
The man you underestimate turns out to be the one you envy
in the end. Never give anyone too much respect, or too little;
there'll always be better people than you, and there'll always be
worse. And you never know who is who, until one of them comes
bombing past you as a sweaty Scooby Doo.

Mark Watson is a stand-up comedian and the author of several novels.

Runners You Know:
The Inexplicably Good Old Runner

A silver-haired sensation, you shatter the egos of younger men as you pass them, effortlessly, at running events. And you know what? I've got a bone to pick with you.

When my partner comes to meet me at the end of half marathons and marathons, bearing an encouraging smile and a goody bag full of refuelling options, he sometimes wonders aloud why I have only just passed the finishing line, staggering away as if I've just run an Ironman Triathlon, while men and women twice my age polished off the race 20 minutes earlier, walking away casually and unruffled.

I normally mumble something about modern science showing that, in fact, running becomes easier as you reach your seventies. He smiles indulgently, pats me on the head and passes me another banana and some coconut water.

But hey, despite the fact they have humiliated me so, I still love the inexplicably good old runners. They are a staple of any big running event, always drawing an extra cheer from spectators, although nobody can work out whether it's patronising to applaud

quite so vigorously. On the other hand, would it be a good idea to call an ambulance, just in case?

The silver strider is likely to wear a laundry-battered oversized T-shirt from a distant running event – say, Budapest Marathon 1978 – that reveals a forest of white hair on their upper arms. These hairs only just conceal the remnants of a fading tattoo, often of an anchor. The women always seem to be really small and hardy looking.

If it's a T-shirt they are sporting, it will often be made out of cotton. For the inexplicably good old runner, technical T-shirts that wick the moisture from the skin are just a myth. They will instead stick stubbornly – and, thanks to sweat – literally, to their cotton T-shirts, come what may.

In his superb book, *The Looniness of the Long Distance Runner*, Russell Taylor writes: 'The problem with cotton is that it is very absorbent and after an hour or so your shirt will be so saturated with sweat that you feel as if you are running in chain mail.' This is true, but maybe these runners enjoy running in chain mail? Perhaps it reminds them of the olden days?

At the 2017 Boston Marathon, 221 of the 27,488 starters were over the age of 70. Long may events everywhere feature the inexplicably good old runners – they are a heart-warming sight and one day, god willing, we will all be one of them.

Unless, that is, we die. Or – far, far worse – live but stop running...

Running Myths Reconsidered:
Barefoot Running is Peak Running

It may be trendy to run barefoot but according to sports performance coach Hannah Schultz: 'For most people, it's just too stressful on the body and on the joints.'

Remember...

You should take at least one, but often two, rest days during the week.

What is the Best Time of Day to Run?

Most runners have a preferred time of day to run. Dawn dashers swear by the early hours, but afternoon addicts point out the clear physical advantages of their choice. Yet for evening evangelists there is nothing better than a run in the dark.

Morning

Pros:

1. It's a good way to wake up for the day.
2. On a primal level it is hugely satisfying to greet dawn in the open air with a burst of physical activity.
3. Your body burns calories faster on an empty stomach, so morning mileage can be a faster track to a flatter stomach.
4. The pavements are quieter, so you can be alone with just your thoughts and the sounds of birds singing, rather than dodging around other runners and wayward toddlers.
5. A study found that morning exercise leads to better sleep quality than afternoon or evening exercise.
6. A morning run gets your daily mileage out of the way early, leaving you free to face the rest of the day with a significant task already achieved, rather than wasting time debating when you'll squeeze it in.
7. Most scientists say that morning is the best time of day to boost muscle.
8. Research from the University of Exeter revealed that 90 per cent of people found their sense of well-being increased after being active outdoors, but sunlight triggers extra serotonin release, so daytime trumps evening.
9. Researchers at the University of Bristol found that a morning workout improved the sharpness of workers and their adeptness at time management. Particularly notable was the workers' confidence that they could handle problems.
10. Dragging yourself from between the sheets and out into a cold, dark morning might not be at all easy but it builds mental strength.

11. You are more likely to hit your targets: research shows that morning exercisers are more consistent with their workout regimes.
12. If you run in the morning, you are more likely to opt for healthier food and lifestyle choices for the rest of the day.
13. Most races and events are held in the morning, so it is very useful to be accustomed to morning running.
14. A study in 2017 found that a morning workout is a habit shared by 59 per cent of active people.

Cons:

1. Lung function is poor in the early hours, so you'll find breathing – and therefore running – considerably harder.
2. If you fall over in the park, how long will it be until someone finds you?
3. Your body temperature is low in the morning, so your muscles are stiff and you're more likely to pick up injury.
4. Statistically, you're also more likely to suffer a heart attack or a stroke in the morning. And that would suck.
5. It's colder.
6. If you've got kids, your partner is unlikely to be thrilled if you're out there pounding the pavement as they get them ready for school. Again.
7. In winter, the pavements are more slippery in the morning. Never mind muscle strains – you could be looking at broken legs if you are not careful.
8. Your immune system is also at its lowest first thing, so as you jog along the pavement you could inadvertently be laying out the red carpet for infection.
9. Early runs can pump you up so much that you become grouchy, which isn't ideal for your morning meeting at work.
10. The rest of the day can stretch long when you've already run several miles before breakfast. All day, whenever you look at the time you find yourself thinking: 'Is that all?'
11. Frankly, you could spend that hour in bed, snuggling under your covers.

Afternoon

Pros:

1. Your body temperature is higher after lunch – for most people in the later afternoon, between 4 p.m. and 5 p.m. – and studies show this higher temperature makes athletes perform better.
2. It's also warmer in the afternoon, which is nice.
3. If you always run during your lunch hour at work, running will never eat into your family time.
4. An early afternoon trot breaks up the day, allowing you some space for thought: how can you make the rest of the day even better?
5. You might find it easier to motivate yourself to get out there once you've been up and about for some hours.

Cons:

1. To make it work, you have to either have an early or a late lunch; just scheduling your food around an afternoon run can be complicated.
2. You're either going to end up having two baths/showers in one day, or be a bit smelly for half the day. Neither scenario is ideal for you, and one of them is far from ideal for those around you.
3. Weather stats show it is more likely to be raining after lunch. Some enjoy a rainy run from time to time, but probably not all the time.
4. An afternoon run on weekends makes any substantial daytime family activity unfeasible. So this, too, can be an unpopular choice for the loved ones of the running fanatic.

Evening

Pros:

1. A dusk round can be a marvellous way to ease out any stresses of the day.
2. While you're running you can't be doing any unhealthy evening activities, such as drinking, binge eating, or boring your loved one with your workplace gripes.
3. There's something rather nice about getting into bed with your muscles tired, and that post-run glow still bright.
4. When it's dark, you get to wear a head torch, and which runner doesn't love a gadget?

Cons:

1. Motivation can be tricky – you put off the run all day and then, come evening, you just might not feel like it after a long day at the office.
2. It's dark out there and there's something a bit depressing about that.
3. It is also unsafe: who is lurking behind that bush, and will that distracted driver see you?
4. Some people find it impossible to sleep after an evening run.
5. It's colder.
6. It's very antisocial: you miss out on a chat with the family, after-work drinks and other social events.

The small print: ultimately, the truth is that the best time of day to run is the time you are most likely to do it.

Remember...

An old Zen saying states: 'You should sit in meditation for 20 minutes every day – unless you're too busy. Then you should sit for an hour.' A similar philosophy can be applied to running. It's very important you get out and run regularly. Unless you don't have time to – in which case it's very, very important you get out and run regularly.

Things We Hate About Running: Experienced Runners Who Dismiss Shorter Distances

We all started somewhere. Just because you have progressed to longer distances and shorter finishing times doesn't mean you should subtly, or less-than-subtly, look down your nose on the progress of newcomers. I remember when I finished my first ever 10k, I could hardly believe I had managed it. When I got to work the next day some old bore snorted when I told him about it, and told me: 'Come back to me when you've done a proper race.' Never be that person.

Run, Forrest Run!

Things People Shout at Runners

Remember...

Dress for how warm you'll feel a mile or two into the run — not for how warm you'll feel in the first mile, when your body is still heating up. Another way of nailing this formula is to dress for runs as if it's 10°C (50°F) warmer than the thermometer actually reads.

Runners You Know: The Unsolicited Coach

Feather-light of build but (when male) heavy of Adam's apple, the unsolicited coach bombards fellow runners with advice at running events. If the runners ignore it, the coach will be deeply hurt. If they benefit from it, he or she will be waiting at the finishing line to say: 'See! See! What did I tell you? What did I tell you, eh?'

When they turn up to club-running get-togethers, they sprint between other runners in order to bestow their wisdom to them, whether anyone asked for it or not. (They usually didn't.)

After the unsolicited coach has completed the course, they stand on the sideline near the finish, bellowing out encouragement and tips to other runners. 'Come on, head up, shoulders square – you can do it!' they tell them. Some advisees are grateful, some are bored, and some don't even hear it, yet the coach offers them all their expertise. They are truly democratic in their avuncular dispensation.

Heck, they might even completely lose control and begin to hang around the local park or riverside, approaching trotters with their tips and wisdom, like jogging Jehovah's Witnesses.

The internet provides a whole new hunting ground for these people to spread their gospel. They can park themselves for hours on online forums, Twitter and Facebook, putting 'right' any runner who has the audacity, the sheer nerve, to approach the pastime in a different way.

If you deign to give another runner advice, you might well find that they are grateful for your input. It might be just what they were hoping for – that breakthrough moment when they ditch a bad habit or adopt a new one, propelling them to future athletic glory. They will always remember you. But there is just as much of a chance that they will see you as an interfering know-it-all. They might not want to be running any faster than they are, they might be very happy plodding away at a steady pace, taking in the scenery and chatting with friends. The last thing they need is a pompous busybody in their face.

So always tread carefully before offering advice. You might find that focusing on your own form is more consistently rewarding in the long run.

Did you Know?

Forty-nine – the age of Belgian runner Stefaan Engels when, in 2011, he set the record for the most consecutive marathons run – 365.

Things We Hate About Running: Tourists

All summer they crowd out streets in city centres and popular towns, inanely meandering around, suddenly stopping dead to gasp at a landmark. Nice for them – hell for anyone trying to run in such an area. For instance, I live near Windsor (also the home of the Queen, don't you know), in England. People often tell me: 'Oh, it must be lovely to run through the town centre in the summer.' It really, really isn't.

Running Myths Reconsidered: Stretching is an Absolute Must

According to experts at the University of Nebraska, stretching isn't as important as once thought, because runners only move their legs in one plane while running. Pre-run stretching can also be detrimental to your performance. The *Journal of Strength and Conditioning Research* went one further, arguing that athletes who performed static stretches had significantly reduced performance and greater energy expenditure compared to those who did not stretch.

Different people will give you differing advice. Ultimately, you can do a lot worse than listening to your body.

Runners You Know: The Quick Starter

You get so excited at the start line of events that you sprint the first 200 metres of the 10k, whereupon you are forced to stop, cough your guts up, and watch as more sensible runners trot past, silently chuckling.

A Guide to Liquid Refreshment

In living memory, runners relied on just water for replenishment. Then runners started to swear by flat cola, before a steady gallop of new products hit the market.

So here's a brief pit stop to give you an overview of the options:

Water

Water may not be seen as sexy and it is not quite as easy to turn it into a commodity, but for the runner, a humble glass of it brings many benefits.

Water will regulate your temperature as you run and help transport nutrients around your body. It also nourishes your cells, lubricates and cushions your joints, and maintains blood volume and pressure.

So, before you are seduced by advertising for sports drinks, gels, electrolyte tablets and other modern products, remember that nature gave us water for a reason. Don't overlook it!

Beetroot (beet) juice

Beetroot juice, or just beet juice if you live in the USA, is growing in popularity for runners. A study by *Runner's World* found that the inorganic nitrate in the juice is converted in your saliva-friendly bacteria into nitrite, which is then converted to nitric oxide, aiding blood flow, muscle contraction, neurotransmission and other important factors for running. In short, it helps your body and mind to fend off exhaustion for longer.

Sports drinks

Filled with sodium, potassium and, most importantly, carbohydrates, sports drinks are a staple part of many runners' on-course intake.

As ultramarathons and triathlons have soared in popularity, endurance sports drinks have entered the commercial fray. Carrying as much as 50 per cent more electrolytes and 25 per cent more carbs, these also include exclusive ingredients, such as multiple transportable carbohydrates, which allow you to absorb even more of the precious stuff.

There are also low- or zero-calorie sports drinks, which offer you the benefits of sports drinks without the calorie onslaught (standard sports drinks typically include around 140kcal).

Running gels

Look at the pavement at any long-distance running event and you will spot shrivelled foil wrappers glistening in the sunshine. To the untrained, or perhaps sweaty, eye, these may look like doomed fish. But they are actually the remnants of energy gels, which help replenish the glycogen and calories runners burn when out on the road. Some runners report digestive distress when they take energy gels, but others swear by these gloopy goodies.

Electrolyte tablets

You can add these to water, bringing sodium, magnesium and calcium to the mix. They will help balance your internal fluids and assist in nutrient absorption, and will also make the water taste interesting and allow you a moment of creativity mid-run.

Did you Know?

Scientists at the University of Northumbria at Newcastle found that drinking 30ml (1fl oz) of cherry concentrate mixed with 100ml (3⅓fl oz) of water twice a day allowed a lower inflammatory response in athletes' muscles. This led to them being able to maintain sprint speed longer than usual.

Notable Runners: Harriette Thompson

In 2017, Harriette became the oldest woman ever to finish a half marathon. She was 94 years of age as she successfully tackled the Synchrony Financial Rock 'n' Roll San Diego Half Marathon. She has beaten cancer twice.

Remember...

The two-day rule states that if something hurts for two straight days while running, you should take two days off. There is also a sibling rule, known as the two-week rule. Here, it is said that if something hurts for two weeks, even if you've taken your rest days, you should seek expert medical help.

Runners You Know: The Relentless Runner

All day every day you are out there, with your spindly physique and leathery skin. No one, not even your family, has ever seen you stationary or fully clothed.

That bad TINDER date is behind you – RUN FAST!

Funny Spectator Signs at Running Events

Things We Hate About Running:
Patronising Commentators

These men – it always seems to be men – who chatter away through the PA at the start/finishing line of big events are all part of the furniture of a race. They can be very encouraging and witty, but they can sometimes be condescending, too. I recall with a shudder one half marathon at which, some hours after the start time, I overheard a commentator saying: 'Give these finishers a special round of applause, they probably don't run very often so make sure you make them feel valued.'

Running Philosophy

❝ Running is the greatest metaphor for life, because you get out of it what you put into it. **❞**

Oprah Winfrey, talk-show host, actress and producer

Runners You Know:
The Disingenuous Dasher

At the starting line of any event, parkrun or club get-together, you say: 'I definitely won't be trying for a personal best, I'm taking it easy today.' However, the moment the starting whistle sounds you sprint off like Usain Bolt with a firework up his ass. You then set a new record, just as you planned all along.

My Running Story: Author Helen Foster

When I run my mind drifts: sometimes it goes in useful places, sometimes it solves my problems, comes up with brilliant ideas, reduces my stress and tackles my woes – most of the time however, it does this ... these are the actual thoughts I noted down one day after a run. Sometimes I wonder about the inside of my head...

1. Right off we go – do I need a jacket? It's chilly.
2. My knee hurts.
3. Still hurting, should I stop?
4. Oh it's alright now.
5. Damn, that means I can't stop, stupid knee.
6. That's a Cornetto wrapper – I haven't had a Cornetto for ages.
7. Don't I run so I CAN eat Cornettos? I think I'll have a Cornetto later – a chocolate one.
8. Actually I guess I'm burning off the wine, beer, spag bol and two scoops of gelato I ate last night.
9. Crap, that's a lot of calories.
10. Left or right?
11. Left is shorter.
12. Left then.
13. No don't open the car door there.
14. Oh FFS snog faster (taps foot and waits).
15. 'I'm just a man, I'm not a hero' – I finished marathon training to this song once. I don't want to run a marathon again. Or do I? Maybe I should enter another marathon – or a half. Maybe just a 10k. Or a fun run.
16. These new shorts are really comfy.
17. I think they're a bit see-through though.
18. That's a big drain hole – I bet there are rats in there.
19. Oh yes, yes, man clomping up behind me, you're running faster than I do, overtake then smartarse.
20. Before you go though, are my shorts a bit see-through?
21. Downhill bit ... I am a unicorn in human form.
22. Yorkshire Terrier alert ... does it look bitey?
23. I don't like little dogs. They scare me. I'll run over here a bit in case it's bitey?
24. Phew ... not bitey.

25. England does have pretty spring flowers.
26. 'Friday, Friday, gotta get down on Friday' – is this REALLY the worst song ever made. I quite like it.
27. Yay, it's the end of my road...
28. I've still got 15 minutes to go.
29. Should have turned right (reverses route).

Helen Foster is a writer specialising in health, nutrition, fitness and beauty. Her books include Gym-spiration: 52 Ways to Wake Up Your Workout *(Health-e Publishing, 2013).*

Notable Runners: Fauja Singh

At the age of 89, Fauja took up running as a hobby to help with grieving after several close relatives died. Four years later, at the age of 93, he set a new record when he completed a marathon in 6 hours and 54 minutes.

Running Philosophy

❝ The true runner is a very fortunate person. He has found something in him that is just perfect. **❞**

George Sheehan, author

Run like United Airlines wants your seat!

Funny Spectator Signs at Running Events

A Brisk Guide to the London Marathon

Like many good ideas, the London Marathon was conceived over a drink in a pub – the Dysart Arms next to Richmond Park just outside London. One of its founders, the late former Olympic champion and journalist Chris Brasher, said of the marathon experience that it sees: 'the human race be one joyous family, working together, laughing together, achieving the impossible'.

The founders also set out six core principles for the London Marathon, of which one was: 'To show mankind that, on occasions, they can be united.'

The first London Marathon duly took place on 29 March 1981. The joint winners were American Dick Beardsley and Norwegian Inge Simonsen. In a lovely gesture, they crossed the finishing line holding hands – in a time of 2:11:48. Not too far behind them was Joyce Smith, a 43-year-old mother of two, who broke the British record to win the women's race, finishing in 2:29:57.

The budget for the inaugural event was £75,000 (aside from any revenue from entry fees). For its first year, more than 20,000 applied to take part, of which 7,747 were accepted and 6,255 crossed the finish line. The following year applications rocketed: more than 90,000 tried to take part. (By 2016, a record total of 247,069 people applied, with around 36,000 starting.)

A funny tale: the night before the race in 1981, former 10,000m world record holder Dave Bedford was in the Mad Hatter, a nightclub in Luton, England. Having sunk several beers, he accepted a bet of £250 that he could not complete the following morning's marathon. He took up the challenge and secured himself a last-minute place, then necked four piña coladas and washed down a king prawn curry with yet another pint of beer. He finally got to bed at 4.45 a.m. Just 75 minutes later he awoke and walked to the London Marathon start. Somehow, he completed the race before falling asleep in a pub. When he got home he spent two days in bed recovering. He would later become a director of the London Marathon.

The first wheelchair marathon was held just two years later, in 1983. Gordon Perry won the men's race in 3:20:07 while his fellow Briton Denise Smith won the women's event in 4:29:03.

In 1985, Matthew Parris MP became the fastest member of parliament to finish the face, polishing it off in an impressive 2:32:57. Some 56 different past or present MPs appeared in the first 34 editions of the race.

During the 11th mile of the mostly flat course, the route passes a little bit of history: runners trot within a few hundred metres/yards of The Mayflower in Rotherhithe, the pub where the Pilgrim Fathers met for a quick pint before they sailed to America.

The event is one of the World Marathon Majors, the six largest and most celebrated marathons in the world. The other five are the Tokyo Marathon, Boston Marathon, Berlin Marathon, Chicago Marathon and New York City Marathon.

The coldest temperature ever was recorded in 1994: 7.6°C (45.7°F).

A separate event, the Polytechnic Marathon, had been held in London since 1909, but it ended in 1996.

Also in 1996 came the hottest temperature to date on race day: an unseasonal 22°C (71.6°F).

In 1998, Mo Farah won the first of three consecutive Mini Marathons, the 3-mile road championship for young athletes aged between 11 and 17 that is held before the main race.

2002 saw 90-year-old Jenny Wood-Allen become the oldest woman to complete a marathon, finishing the course in 11 hours and 34 minutes. She took part despite injuring her head in a training fall.

The London Marathon attracts plenty of runners in fancy dress. Perhaps the most notable example came in 2002, when Lloyd Scott wore a deep-sea diving suit that weighed a total of 50kg (110lb) – each of his shoes weighed 11kg (24lb). Unsurprisingly, he also set a record for the slowest London Marathon time – 5 days, 8 hours, 29 minutes and 46 seconds!

However, current regulations state that the race must be completed within 24 hours.

In 2006, two participants – Katie Austin and Gordon Frye – got married on Tower Bridge during the run.

There are around 1.25 million bottles of water and energy drinks along the route, with 600 trestle tables for the feed stations located at every mile marker.

In 2007, 22-year-old David Rogers became the ninth marathon runner to die after the race – he had drunk too much water.

However, in 2008, a heart-warming story emerged: Buster Martin became the oldest runner to complete the race. He claimed to be 101 years old, though this was later disputed. Whatever the case, his first words as he slid past the finish line were 'Where's my beer?'

Kenyan Sammy Wanjiru became the youngest male winner in 2009, crossing the line at the age of 22. Tragically, he died two years later after falling from a balcony.

The most common profession for those taking part is teaching. However, among the other occupations are scientists, nurses, taxi drivers, electricians and burlesque dancers.

Virgin took over sponsorship in 2011. Sir Richard Branson said: 'It's the single biggest fundraising day on the planet and we want to make it even bigger.'

In the same year, a football freestyler completed the 26.2 miles while kicking a ball up between his right and left foot with each step. He did not drop the ball once, but it took him a while to get round the course. He eventually finished in 12 hours 15 minutes.

People try to break peculiar records. In 2014 alone, individuals attempted to achieve the accolade of the 'fastest man dressed as a toilet', or to complete the 'fastest marathon carrying golf clubs' and 'fastest marathon in high heels'.

Over 1 million runners completed the London Marathon between 1981 and 2016, with a record 39,140 people finishing in 2016.

Remember...

If it's looking icy and slippery out there, it can be very, very unwise to 'chance it' and set out for a run. Stay at home, or drive to the gym and use the treadmill. Many gyms offer day passes. Yes, treadmills are boring, but so are broken legs after a while.

Running Philosophy

❝ If you are losing
faith in human nature,
watch a marathon. **❞**

Kathrine Switzer, the first woman to run the Boston Marathon as an
official entrant, as well as being an author and TV commentator

Things We Hate About Running: Expos

Why (oh why) would you conveniently post someone their
running number for an event through the mail when you can
demand that they attend a soulless, hectic, crowded, germ-
infested commercialised gathering a day or so before the biggest
run of their life? I mean to say, what else would anyone want to
be doing 24 hours before a marathon than squeezing their way
through stressed-out crowds at an expo centre?

Things People Shout at Runners

Remember...

It is really nice to smile and thank the volunteers at races.
Wave back to the crowds who are spurring you on. Bask in
the moment!

Runners You Know:
The Social Media Bore

'How do you know if someone has run a marathon?' begins the old joke. 'Answer: they'll tell you.' Well, the social media bore takes this truism about the one-off bragging of the runner and turns it into a daily affair.

It's odd to think that, within the lifetime of many who are reading this book, there was an era in which the runner kept the minutiae of his or her daily jogs and weekly mileage largely to themselves.

After all, very few people are terribly interested in other people's daily runs. That much is obvious to most of us, but not the social media bore. 'Morning everyone!' they post on Facebook at 7 a.m. on a Saturday. 'Just ran 24 miles at an average pace of 8:06. #running #amrunning #thankful'.

Bubbling over with post-run enthusiasm, the social media bore genuinely believes this news will absolutely mesmerise their friends on Facebook and Twitter. They can picture their friends smiling with fascinated joy as this update pops up on their feed.

Online narcissism is a part of many people's lives. Runners merely have their own take on it. Applied for a marathon place? Announce this online. Get accepted for the marathon? Inform your friends and followers instantly. Receive your race number? Take a photograph and show it to everyone online. Start your training? Again, announce it. And then catalogue every single training run, month after month, as you count down to the big day.

And by the time that day comes, your friends are absolutely exhausted by your incessant marathon updates. They could be forgiven for thinking that, for you, running is less about running, and more about pumping out a non-stop commentary.

That said, don't lose too much sleep over it all. If you've been prattling away about running on Facebook and Twitter for any length of time, most of your friends and followers have probably quietly muted your updates and tweets yonks ago, leaving you bragging into a vacuum.

My Running Story:
Author Vybarr Cregan-Reid

When I was writing my book about running, I discovered some obvious things about how it makes us fitter or stronger. But when I started to look behind the curtain, at all the magical things that happen in our bodies because we run, I discovered some truly amazing stuff: running can make us better at our jobs, more empathetic, it can help us solve problems more quickly, makes us a better friend or partner and, best of all, it actually makes us more intelligent. I wrote about all of these in *Footnotes*, but one of the unbelievably effective technologies that I didn't get round to discussing was the sheer magic of that thing that all runners do when they pound the hills, roads and tracks: sweat.

It turns out that our success as a species is due to 1 per cent inspiration, 99 per cent perspiration. Without this absolutely amazing technology we would not have climbed our way to the top of the evolutionary pile. Many animals perspire, but no others use it as such an efficient and refined cooling technology.

We often assume that it is our brainpower that differentiates us from other animals. It is obvious that we are able to process more intellectual stimuli than other mammals, but any PC-owner knows that computational power is completely useless if the cooling system fails. And this is what really sets us apart: our ability to maintain an effective working temperature, not just so that we can keep moving, but so that we can keep thinking while in motion, efficiently chasing down the quarry.

As a species, over short distances, we are hopeless runners. We might be able to go a long way but what use is that if we can't catch anything? The truth is that we never could if it weren't for several factors that make us identifiably human, and it is our ability to perspire that renders them all effective. So, we may have perfect bodies for distance running, but those features that enable us to move so effectively are useless without correct temperature control.

There are distinct thermoregulatory advantages to being a two-legged human. Being merely upright, for example, means that less of the sun hits you when it's at its hottest. The bipedal human exposes only about 7 per cent of their surface area to sunlight; it is triple this for a quadruped. This fact alone means that being on two legs enables you to move with greater heat efficiency. Also, by being upright, we can take advantage of the fact that our brains are further away from the harsher micro-climate found at ground level, which is hotter because it is heated by the sun and because there is less air movement there.

Moreover, with the air movement found away from the ground comes evaporation, which is the real miracle technology. Evaporation is such an effective way to lose heat that if 1 litre (2 pints) of sweat is able to evaporate on the surface of your skin, you can lose about half a million calories of heat in the process.

Most quadrupeds sweat – in order to maintain skin health and create scent (we do this, too), and even to create ear wax (which, surprisingly, is also a sort of sweat) – but for thermoregulation, most animals use interior air movement (panting) to cool down. This means their bodies have to actively work to lose heat, unlike ours. So, on a hot day, we can potentially chase down a quadruped until it starts to overheat, and when it stops to shed some heat we humans can keep going and close the gap a little. Eventually, the distance between predator and prey will close as their technology fails and ours keeps functioning. Sweat means that we are much better hunters than we appear to be.

It is decidedly odd that sweat is taboo in our society. Do it in the wrong place or from the wrong part of your body and the people around you will become uncomfortable, or at the very least make you feel so ... and that will probably make you sweat.

If you sweat on a run it's aesthetic – a badge of honour, part of the training montage of any sports movie you might think of. But get it wrong – sweat in a job interview, presentation or social situation – and people will think you've lost control, or that it's a stress response because you are deceiving them. Yet without it we would never have become who we are, have survived to the point when we could invent things, create art, make music or write.

So, if you struggle a bit in the heat, think of those beads of sweat on your forehead, and the fact that the exposed skin there, and its ability to perspire, is what keeps your brain functioning. In the past, it made you a lethal weapon out on the savannah, now it might allow you to reflect on what it has allowed you to achieve in the past, and that without those 2.5 million sweat glands on your skin working to maintain the correct temperature for thought, you would not be here, reading this.

Vybarr Cregan-Reid is the author of Footnotes: How Running Makes Us Human (Ebury, 2017).

Things We Hate About Running: The Non-Transfer of Places Rule

Why, if a runner falls ill or has to drop out of a fully booked race, should they not be allowed to transfer their unwanted place to another runner who is desperate to take part? Most big events flatly refuse to allow such transfers, which means everyone loses out. The ill runner is out of pocket for an event they cannot take part in, the runner who can't get a place loses out, and the event itself misses a chance to have a full turnout. Come on, organisers – you could even profit from transfers by charging a small admin fee!

Remember...

Never answer an email or text message in the first hour after a long run. The chances of you firing off a narky or overly frank reply are high until the adrenalin settles.

Did you Know?

Thirty per cent – the reduction in risk of erectile dysfunction in a study in the *Annals of Internal Medicine* among men who ran 'vigorously' several times a week.

The Trouble With Sitting

Even runners need to take the weight off their feet, but sitting down brings a series of dangers for the athletically inclined. This is because when seated your circulation slows down and your fat burners switch off. Muscles in the hip flexors, hamstrings and lower back tighten, while muscles in other parts of the body overwork, risking injury.

A study published in the *American Journal of Epidemiology* found that women who sit for 10 hours or more each day age faster than those who exercise daily. Telomeres, which are chromosome-protecting caps, naturally shorten with age, but researchers found that they shorten faster among the sedentary half of the research field, making such women biologically eight years older than the exercising half. Sitting for long periods has also been linked to type II diabetes, obesity and cancer.

A study published in *Frontiers in Human Neuroscience* found that the brains of distance runners had different connections in areas known to assist sophisticated cognition from those found in the brains of healthy but sedentary people.

For this reason, it is important that desk-bound runners – and indeed non-runners – should build in regular walk breaks. Alternatively, you could use an adjustable standing desk – they're all the rage right now.

Funny Spectator Signs at Running Events

Running Philosophy

❝ Some sessions are stars and some are stones, but in the end they are all rocks and we build upon them. **❞**

Chrissie Wellington, OBS, British triathlete
and four-time Ironman Triathlon World Champion

Runners You Know: The Ninja

Most running gear nowadays comes in fairly bright and garish colours. Take a look at the pack at any race or event and it will be like a bag of kids' candy – all bright orange, screaming green and attention-hungry yellow.

There are also luminous and reflector accessories, to make it safer for runners (and the rest of the world) when they jog in dark conditions. So most runners will be seen long before they are heard, and the world is all the safer for this fact.

However, the ninja runner stands against this trend. They wear sombre clothes from head to toe, meaning that on a dark morning or any time after sunset they will fade into the background. This makes them dangers to themselves and others, since they could bump into another person, or a car could bump into them, at any point.

No one is quite sure why the ninjas insist on dark clothing. Is it because black is said to be slimming? Do they think it makes them look dramatic? Or are they hoping a passing film director will cast them as a sexy assassin?

Either way, they make for a menacing presence – you just never know when they will suddenly appear out of the shadows.

Did you Know?

Fifty – the average number of breaths you take per minute when you run – compared to 15 when you rest.

Things We Hate About Running: Full Fools

There's something strangely unsettling about runners who, when discussing a marathon, use the term 'full marathon' or just 'full' to refer to it. As if, should they fail to include the 'f' word, mass confusion will break out.

A similar pest is the non-runner who assumes that any marathon apart from London or New York will be of a shorter length.

Me: 'I ran the Dublin Marathon.'

Them: 'Oh right, how long is that one?'

Me: '...'

Funny Spectator Signs at Running Events

Runners You Know: The Splasher

While everyone else carefully runs around puddles, you never saw a single puddle you didn't want to gallop straight through, as if you're the subject of some clichéd equine portrait. It's such fun!

My Running Story: Broadcaster Nicky Campbell

I love to run. I need to run. I wish I could run like I used to run. The days of 62-minute 10-milers are far behind me and all the other runners are way in front of me, but still I drag myself out of the house after a mentally exhausting four-hour stint on the radio (no, believe me, it is!) and let my mind fly.

Seb Coe once used a memorable phrase when I asked him if he had any tips for running a mile. 'Keep to your pace for the first half of the race and then in the last 800 – let your mind fly'.

Letting your mind fly – it's a powerful, wonderful and even for the clunkier of bog-standard joggers, recognisable feeling. Don't you know just what he means?

The body and mind are invigorated and thoughts flow like a river in spate. It's as if the creative waterways are free again. Why didn't I think of that earlier? Yes – that's what to say – that's what to do – that's the answer. John Lennon sang about 'Instant Karma'. Well, running gives you guaranteed 'Eureka'.

I push and I creak. I groan and I heave my still-slight but soon-to-be 56-year-old frame and I never regret it. Who ever thought it would come to this though? A mere 8 kilometres (5 miles) feels like an Iron Man these days.

I was the best in my year at school and as an average rugby player this gave my dad something to be proud of. I still get emotional as I write that. It was only when I was running round Wandsworth Common in London when I was in my late 30s that I became aware that I had a rather unconventional and un-Coe-like running style. It lacked his, shall we say, 'effortless elegance'. I realised this on one fateful day when some lads I drifted past laughed and referred to me as Forrest Gump. Since then, whenever I run past a shop window I glance sideways and my heart sinks a bit. It's rather like the voice you think you have, compared to the one you hear on a recording – not nearly as good. That's a heavy burden for a radio presenter. Trust me.

One evening many years ago I was out running on a beautiful summer's evening past the multi-million-pound old terrace houses of Highgate Village and I 'Gumped' past a man at a gate enjoying the balmy evening air. I clocked him and as I ran the next

100 metres (100 yards) I worked out exactly who he was. Stopping to look back at the end of the road I had a feeling of dread. I was right. He had come out on to the road and was staring at me intently. It was Tom Hanks.

For some considerable time in subsequent years, I began to entertain the theory and indeed fear that Forrest Gump was actually based on me... However, the timings didn't quite fit when I worked out where I was living and when. What actually happened was perhaps even more bizarre. Hanks saw a man running like Forrest Gump and must have thought I was performing some strange homage – he did look utterly intrigued and totally mystified. Tom does intrigued and mystified like no one else, believe me. This was long before selfies, but you know what? I would probably have let him have one.

I rounded the corner, ran down to Hampstead Heath and let my mind fly.

Nicky Campbell is one of Britain's most distinguished broadcasters. Over the past four decades he has presented Wheel of Fortune, Watchdog, Long Lost *and* Big Questions.

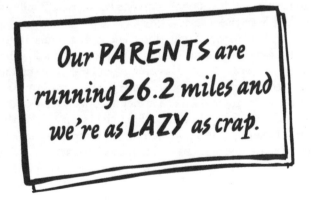

Funny Spectator Signs at Running Events

Running Philosophy

❝ If you want to win something,
run 100 metres. If you want
to experience something,
run a marathon. **❞**

Emil Zátopek, triple-gold medallist in
the 1952 Helsinki Olympics

Runners You Know: The Parkrun Tourist

If you spot a car driving ponderously through your area at
8.34 a.m. on a Saturday morning, with a pair of gaunt faces
peering curiously out of the windows, the chances are you've just
seen some parkrun tourists.

Having vowed to take part at every parkrun in the country,
they spend their Saturday mornings bombing along motorways
and then inching around town centres. Barcodes safely tucked
in their shorts' key pocket, they then emerge into yet another
unfamiliar park. The contours of the venue might be foreign
to them, they may not understand the in-jokes of the pre-run
briefing, and they won't recognise any of their fellow parkrunners,
but do they mind? Not a bit! For these people the unfamiliarity of
it all is a key component of parkrun tourism. They will run their
5k, get their finishing token and barcodes scanned, and then bask
in the satisfaction as they tick off another location on the parkrun
map. They really are going to conquer the country, one parkrun
at a time.

When the run is done with, they either return down the
motorway to their homes, or, if further afield in an interesting
area – a seaside idyll or somesuch – they might hang around and
take in the sights. Let the cynics sneer and giggle about 'saddos'
all they like – the parkrun tourists love what they do, and there
are far, far worse ways to spend a weekend.

Running Myths Reconsidered: Dehydration and Electrolyte Loss Cause Cramp

In 2011, *British Journal of Sports Medicine* researchers compared blood electrolyte and hydration levels of two groups of triathletes: those who suffered from cramp and those who did not. They found no differences and concluded that cramping was actually the result of increased running speed.

Remember...

When you have a cold, if the symptoms are all above the chest, you can still run. If they have moved into your chest, stay at home.

Runners You Know: Bandana Guy

To wear a bandana, it seems to be necessary for you to also be in your 60s, and for you to have a greying goatee. Facial piercings are popular too, as are body tattoos.

Your bandana will usually depict the stars and stripes of the American flag, some sort of rock insignia, or else something related to Harley Davidsons or Jack Daniels.

No one is quite sure why, but there always seems to be at least one of you at every running event – from mass-participation marathons to small, intimate parkruns. You are truly part of the running community and we all wish you well as you rock out in life. Eighteen till you die, dude!

Did you Know?

In 2004, a team of sports scientists lead by Kenyatta University studied a group of 10 leading Kenyan male distance runners. They found that for these elite runners a surprisingly large 20 per cent of their calories came from refined sugars. This compared unfavourably with the equivalent percentage among average Brits. For them, just 12 per cent came from refined sugar. The reasons for the Kenyans' high percentage? Their love of sugary tea.

May the COURSE be with you.

Funny Spectator Signs at Running Events

Running Wisdom

" I've been to 'real' therapy, too, and for me, nothing beats running. It is truly the best therapy. I connect to my father and talk through things as if he were there. I don't have my dad to talk to in real life, but he's there with me when I run. **"**

An unnamed son of a 9/11 victim, quoted in *The New Yorker*

The Ten Commandments of Running Etiquette

1. Dress appropriately

Chaps, in your head you may have the torso of a *Men's Health* cover star, but the chances are that your body hasn't got that memo. So please try to avoid running tops that reveal more than anyone wants to see – and don't even think of going topless.

2. Keep it clean

Whether you are running alone through the park or at a big event manned by stewards and other volunteers, please dispose of your empty water bottles and gel wrappers responsibly. Runners enjoy nature more than many types of people, so let's protect, rather than destroy, it.

3. Consider your sweat

As you work up a sweat during a run you can feel wonderfully alive and vital, connected with your very godly essence. But to the rest of the world you're just a big smelly sod. So don't get too much in other people's space until you've showered and changed.

4. Face the traffic

Always run against the flow of traffic – doing this will reduce your chances of being scraped off the pavement.

5. Be thankful

When you are running at an event, it's lovely to thank the water station team and other volunteers. Even a simple smile as you grab the water bottle goes a long way for these people who work so hard.

6. Check before you spit

Sometimes during a run you will need to spit, or even empty your nostrils. It's rather nice to make sure you are not about to expel it straight into the path of another runner, or general passer-by.

7. Three's a crowd

When you're out running with your local club, you might like to catch up with your mates. This is fine, but running more than two abreast is simply antisocial and boorish.

8. Freshen up in private

We've all seen this runner. At the starting line, he (come on, it's always he) applies lube to his nipples and upper thighs in front of everyone. Soon after finishing, he lifts up his T-shirt and sprays cheap deodorant over his armpits. Don't be that guy. Just don't.

9. Keep your little one close

If you are running with a dog, keep them on a tight leash. If you are running with a pram, don't force it into the paths of other runners. Yes, they will feel obliged to get out of the way, but using your child in this way is a bit creepy.

10. Keep moving at the finish

When you cross the finish line, keep moving forwards. The runner who suddenly stops at this point risks causing an annoying and dangerous pile-up, ruining the big moment for themselves and everyone else.

Did you Know?

A survey in 2015 delved into what underwear – if any – female runners wear when out jogging. The study found that 11 per cent of female Canadian runners run without any underwear, with 8 per cent of American women admitting to the same practice. It was a different story in Germany – there, some 72 per cent of women respondents said they wear granny panties.

Runners You Know: The Thirsty One

Drinks stations at running events can be chaotic affairs. Earnest volunteers offer up lidless plastic bottles or flimsy plastic cups of water as pumped-up runners whizz past. Runners bump into one another, drinks are accidentally spilt – it can be a (quite literally) thankless task for the volunteers.

But for the thirsty runner, this is one of their favourite parts of the whole day. Nearly as dependent on regular water as your average fish, these people are perpetually gasping. They really set up camp at the water station, grabbing several cups and necking them straight down, before taking another and throwing it over their face. As they set off, they might even seize another to take with them – one for the road, and all that.

Not that water stops are the only time these runners drink. They often carry with them a personal, hand-held water bottle to tide them over between the official stations. The particularly thirsty runner might even have a camel pack – the aqua-filled backpack. It all seems a little excessive for a mere 10k on a cool day.

Why are these people so thirsty? Surely they shouldn't be running around their local park, but instead, hotfooting it to their local doctor for an urgent diabetes test. Either that, or consuming less salt.

Dehydration is something to avoid when you're running, but so is over-hydration. If as you run your midrift is making sloshing sounds as all that water flies around, then you might have overdone it a touch.

After all, experts suggest we only need to take in 150–350ml (5–12fl oz) of fluid every 15–20 minutes during the run, so unless you have an extreme condition, it is probably safe to rely on the water stations alone.

My Running Story: Author Amy Alward

When I was preparing for the 2012 Edinburgh Marathon, I realised that training for a marathon is a lot like writing a novel...

1. You need the right gear ... but gear won't do the work for you!
    Yes, you need the right kit to run: properly fitted trainers, clothes that wick away sweat, maybe a heart-rate monitor so you can judge the improvements in your fitness... they will all help to better your training. But you can get carried away – Nike+ or a GPS running watch? Barefoot running shoes or comfortable, sturdy Asics? You can get carried away with writing gadgets too. Plain Microsoft Word or Scrivener? Fountain pen or ballpoint? Laptop? iPad? Spiral notebook?

    To start running you really just need a pair of running shoes, some clothes you can sweat in, and the road. Just like all you really need to write is good old pen and paper. You can't let the pursuit of perfect gear prevent you from starting.

2. There are no shortcuts
    When training for a marathon, you gotta put in the miles. There's just no getting around it. Yes, when I ran to work I was sometimes tempted to detour toward the bus stop where I could hop on a vehicle that would take me straight to the office. But I knew that that was not going to help me on marathon day. Same with writing a novel – you have to put the words down on paper, or else you're never going to end up with a finished product.

3. Sometimes you feel you're not getting anywhere
    I was running anywhere between 32 and 48 kilometres (20 and 30 miles) per week but when it came to getting fitter, sometimes I felt like I wasn't getting anywhere. Some runs are just plain hard, and I don't understand why my body will scream against a 6.5 kilometre (4 mile) run when it happily endured 13 kilometres (8 miles) the week before. Writing feels like that sometimes. There are periods when I feel like my writing is not getting any better (it might even be getting worse!), and the finish line feels further away than it ever did before.

The only solution to this, I've found, is to switch it up. Instead of a run, I jump on the cross-trainer at the gym, or go to the climbing wall with a work friend. Instead of forcing myself to write another paragraph on *Oathbreaker 2*, I'll do a freeform writing exercise, or update the blog, or read a book to get inspired.

4. You need to have the proper fuel

    In order to run, you have to fuel your body properly. My pre-run breakfast consists of porridge and a banana – boring, but it works! And for any run longer than about 9.5 kilometres (6 miles), I take a bottle of orange-flavour Lucozade Sport. You also have to pay attention to what you eat and drink to get you through your writing days.

5. There will be pain

    I've actually been fairly lucky when it comes to running injuries and (touch wood) I've never experienced anything that has been completely debilitating. That doesn't mean there hasn't been pain, however! Pain in muscles I didn't even know I had. Soreness that won't disappear for days, blisters in between my toes, twinges in my knees and beside my shin bone. In writing, there is pain too. The pain of rejection – injuring the pride you didn't even really know you had – the agony of not being able to solve a plot point in a storyline that you created, the reviews that cut to the bone ... oh yes, and the most common of writing ailments: the dreaded papercut! Sometimes those sting really bad, man...

6. Reactions

   When you complete a marathon or a novel, people's reactions can be similar. Friends, family and complete strangers will marvel, and say that they could never do a thing like that … they couldn't run a mile, or they couldn't dream of putting down that many words. But what they don't realise is that to achieve those goals you just have to put in the miles, put in the sweat, put in the tears.

   Or at the very least, give it a go. And if it's not a marathon or a whole novel yet, start with a 10k race or a short story. For every writing or running journey, you gotta start somewhere.

Amy Alward is the author of The Potion Diaries (Simon & Schuster Children's UK, 2015) *(@amy_alward)*

Things We Hate About Running: Hangovers

As a tee-totaller, I feel I should be able to bask in a life free from the hell of hangovers. Except that as a runner, I run the risk of dehydration hangovers if I forget to rehydrate properly after a long or hot run. And the vulnerable truth is that as I stagger through the door after a baking 18-miler, I do sometimes forget to take in water. So despite being booze free, I have the same pounding headache the next morning.

I have a CAB fare.

Funny Spectator Signs at Running Events

Runners You Know: The Traditionalist

Running clothes are evolving at a sprinting pace, but you stubbornly stick to your old-school cotton tracksuit combo, complete with sweatbands around your wrists and head. You basically look like you've jogged out of a classic '80s Jane Fonda video.

Remember...

The most effective training imitates the event for which you are preparing.

Things We Hate About Running: Slow Runners Who Line Up at the Front of the Pack

This is a selfish move. Lining up with the faster runners may mean you get away from the starting line more quickly, but if you aren't planning to run at their pace you're just being selfish. Position yourself accurately.

Things People Shout at Runners

Perfecting Your Posture

With so much emphasis on fitness and stamina, posture can be an overlooked aspect of efficient running. Here are the key tips for getting it right:

1. You should look ahead with your eyes and head up. Don't succumb to the temptation to look down since this will make you lean forwards, adding to the strain on your lower back. Looking up will also mean you can see where you are going, and breathe better.
2. If you scan the horizon this should automatically straighten your neck and back and bring them into alignment.
3. Your mouth should be relaxed and open. This will aid your breathing, which will get more of that all-important oxygen into you.
4. This is a key one – keep your shoulders down. Many runners instinctively hunch and tense their shoulders, but this is a waste of energy during the run and can lead to muscular strains after it. Drop and soften the shoulders. Relax them. They'll thank you for it.
5. Hands should be kept in an unclenched fist. Your arms should predominantly swing forwards and back, rather than across the body, between waist and lower-chest level. Bend your elbows at a 90-degree angle.
6. Hip abduction increased by 10 per cent in a study that the University of Memphis conducted into the effects of fatigue during long runs. So keep your hips high by imagining yourself staying tall and maintaining a level pelvis.
7. The hips area is a key one to make sure you are holding yourself upright. You should lean forwards at your ankles instead of your waist, or you will diminish your breathing and blood flow to the muscles.
8. Force production in the quads has been found to drop by 26 per cent on long runs. Avoid this by making sure the leg does not sink over the foot.

Runners You Know: The Pram-Pusher

You run with your toddler strapped into a pushchair in front of you. As you cross the finish line together the kid is either crying or vomiting. And so are you.

Weird Marathons: Man v Horse Marathon

One evening in a Welsh pub, two revellers were discussing whether a human or a horse would win in a race. The pub landlord decided to put the matter to the test, and thus was born the Man v Horse marathon. The rival species line up each year to compete over the course in Britain's smallest town (or so it claims), Llanwrtyd Wells. A horse won for the first 24 years of the contest, until an elite British marathon runner, Huw Lobb, became the race's first human victor.

Ingredients for a Perfect Parkrun

It's the Saturday-morning fitness phenomenon that swept Britain and has now spread far and wide. Each week, more than 70,000 runners line up at parkrun: the free, timed 5k runs that take place in parks across Britain and many other places besides – there are now parkruns in 15 countries across five continents.

As anyone who has run at more than one parkrun venue will tell you, each has its own plus points and drawbacks. So here is a (somewhat personal and subjective) guide to the perfect parkrun.

Start/finish area

Having the start and finish area in the same location is a joy. Runners can leave belongings there and relax in the knowledge that someone will always be keeping an eye on them. It also simplifies matters for any family or friends who have come along to cheer on their running loved one. They can watch them set out and return, without having to move.

A fast course

This means a nice flat surface, with minimal twists and turns. Keep it flat and let the runners whizz along it on their way to new PBs and the inherent glory. There is a mental dimension to this, too. All parkrun courses are 5k, but I am both joking and not joking when I say that some seem two or three times longer than others.

Simplicity rules

Just as a single lapper is important, so is a simple course. Anyone who has attended a pre-run briefing knows that the course will be described for the benefit of any newcomers. The longer the description goes on, the more complicated the course will be. Nobody has gone along in search of an orienteering experience, full of twists, turns and backtracks. Who wants to be concentrating on the route, when they could be concentrating on the run?

We do like to be beside the seaside

Coastal runs are something special. Running with the salt air filling your lungs and the breathtaking views of the ocean – marvellous!

The beauty of nature

A picturesque course always goes down well, doesn't it? Plenty of greenery, water and wildlife provide a beautiful backdrop to an enjoyable parkrun. Ponds, lakes, streams and rivers are not just pretty to look at, but they also produce a cleaner feel to the air that pumps in and out of your lungs as you run around. If there are ducks, swans and geese living on them, then all the better. It is a tremendous privilege to monitor the passing of the seasons as you run around your local park. You can watch the leaves and flowers emerge in spring, and fall in autumn. You can wave farewell to the birds as they fly off for warmer pastures, and welcome them back as the temperatures perk up in late spring.

Clear, permanent markers

When organisers are permitted to install permanent kilometre markers and arrows along the course, it makes it easier for everyone. Newcomers or occasional attendees can easily monitor their progress and keep up with the course, and volunteers are saved the weekly effort of trudging around the course to put out, and then collect, temporary signs.

Toilets

When you've got to go, you've got to go. A lack of facilities in a park only leads to risky squatting and other unsightly barbarities. So parks with a loo will always win out over their facility-lacking siblings.

It's a dog's life

Again, this one is subjective. Some runners absolutely hate having dogs involved in the parkrun. Even when, as per the rules, the running dogs are kept on a tight leash, they are enough to annoy, unsettle or even terrify some runners. However, for others, the presence of our four-legged friends is an important ingredient of a good parkrun experience. To line up at the start alongside a different species, and then to run alongside them, in pursuit of the same goal, may be tremendously moving.

Cafe culture

Friendlier runners can network and refuel after the run if there is a cafe. When a regular has a birthday or passes the 100 parkruns milestone, there can be cakes and speeches there. If it's raining before the run, parkrunners can gather inside until 9 a.m. Cafes really are an important part of parkrun.

Wide, open paths

I once travelled to an unfamiliar parkrun. On the day, I decided I would really put my foot down on the course, and hopefully get a PB. I warmed up carefully, psyched myself up, and even necked a caffeine pill to give me an extra kick. I was pumped...

... and then I reached the starting line, and realised that for the first kilometre at least, the path would be so narrow and crowded that we would be lucky to get much beyond brisk walking pace. I was more or less grinding my teeth with frustration as we inched along, with prams and dogs also jammed into the pack.

Give us a nice broad path, so there is room for everyone and we can all run at our chosen pace.

The right crowd size

This is more a matter of personal taste. Some runners like a big field of parkrunners. Bushy Park in London, for instance, regularly attracts more than 1000. Other runners prefer a really small group, where it is more intimate, where you can get an impressive-sounding finishing position almost by default, and where things are generally less crowded and intense.

Whatever your preference, this is a more important factor than many realise. So check the figures before you set out to a new park, so you know what is in store for you.

Dry

Some winters get very, very wet in the UK and elsewhere, so a venue that won't turn into a flooded lagoon at the first sign of the wet stuff is preferable. It's parkrun, not parkswim!

Quick results

Some parkruns will post race times within an hour of the final runner crossing the line. Others take several hours or most of the day. While the efforts of all are voluntary and appreciated, you cannot beat the feeling of getting your results through quickly.

Kindly organisers

Most parkrun volunteers and organisers are absolutely lovely, true angels for our time. However, just occasionally you find one for whom their parkrun involvement is the most power they've ever had in their life. They greet it by strutting around self-righteously with their clipboards, reminding everyone of the rules and generally snarling at runners like we are naughty children.

Some of the aforementioned bores also police people's conversations. If they overhear someone talk about who won the run, they'll march up to remind them: 'Excuse me, there is no winner, only a first finisher' or 'Erm, remember it's not a race – it's you against the clock'.

Luckily, you are unlikely to come upon these people, since they are very much in the minority in the generally joyful parkrun family.

A good car park

This is rather self-explanatory, isn't it? No one wants to arrive at a parkrun and find themselves crawling around local streets looking for somewhere to leave their car, all the while worrying that they will miss the start time. For parkrun tourists, this is an even more important feature. While we're in wish-list mode, it's also very nice indeed when the car park is free of charge. Yay for nice car parks!

Attractive runners

This is not a feature that many parkrunners will admit to prioritising. At least not out loud. However, there is no doubt that a field of runners containing a few shapely beauties or honed Adonises is no bad thing. It has been known for a particularly agreeable figure to somehow drag other runners to a personal best, as they scramble to keep up with the heavenly sight in front of them. It's rather awkward, jolly inappropriate, and very, very true.

A concise briefing

The pre-run briefing is an important feature of the parkrun experience. The run director grabs a loud hailer and, stepping up on a bench, milk crate or other improvised stage, runs through a number of preliminaries. The volunteers are thanked, visiting runners are welcomed, personal milestones are celebrated, and more. There are also announcements and other formalities, before, in theory at least, the run sets off at 9 a.m. sharp.

Unfortunately, for some briefers, the experience rather goes to their head. They will attempt jokes, offer irrelevant information, and explore time-consuming irrelevance such as whether any runners have a birthday or special occasion coming up.

Before you know it, it is far beyond the official start time. This may seem a trivial matter, but for those who have warmed up carefully for a 9 a.m. start, perhaps in the hope of getting a PB, it is increasingly frustrating as the briefer milks their moment in the spotlight. The same goes for those who are incorporating the 5k of the parkrun into a much longer morning run. Having timed their arrival carefully in the hope of a seamless flow into the parkrun, it is annoying to stand kicking their heels as a loud hailer-wielding director makes 'funny' remarks about it being nice weather for ducks.

One lap is wonderful

Multi-lap parkruns are sometimes inevitable. Either the park is too small to incorporate a single-lap 5k, or the local authorities have only allowed run organisers access to one small part of the park.

However, while such obstacles are understandable, there is little doubt that the best parkruns are those that consist of just a single lap. This keeps the scenery fresh throughout the course and avoids runners having to engage in mid-run mathematics: 'Am I on my second or third lap? Please be the third! Drat, it's only the second!'

Another issue with multi-lappers is that the distance signs throughout the course become horribly confusing. Three minutes into a run you find yourself passing a sign that says '3km' and you wonder whether you've gone mad. You haven't. You're just at the wrong parkrun.

Friendly – but not too friendly – regulars

It's lovely when the regulars at any parkrun are welcoming. It's nice to think that, as you run together throughout the seasons, you have one another's backs. But this can go too far. When I stopped going to my local for a while, I found that whenever I bumped into parkrunners out and about in town they would interrogate me incredulously over why I'd stopped going. 'But what do you MEAN you won't be coming for a while?' they would ask, all watery eyed and confused. Friendly is good. Cultish is creepy.

Runners You Know: The Angry Runner

In your case, your every run is powered by how indignant you are. And how indignant are you? WELL, VERY INDIGNANT INDEED, THANK YOU VERY MUCH!

Often a middle-aged man (some would say *always* a middle-aged man), you are one who seethes, sighs and jostles through every run. You roll your eyes so much while you're out there it's a wonder you don't bump into things.

Of course, if you were to bump into anything you would take this as yet more evidence of how the world is going to hell in a handbasket. Life is a mystery to you: what on earth is wrong with everyone, you find yourself asking. You probably have passionate views on the rise of populism in politics.

Everything seems to make you angry. When you train, you cannot believe that people have the gall, the sheer nerve, to be out walking on the pavements and in the parks at the same time as you chose to go out and run. What is that all about?

As you weave your way through the selfish strollers you make sure to pass as closely as possible to them, all the better to intimidate them. You might even huff or tut as you pass, to remind them of how unreasonably they're behaving. Fancy walking around their local park on a Saturday morning! Disgusting!

At running events you get even more angry. There's so much to seethe about! The crowded field in the first kilometre or so is classic Angry Runner territory. The people running slowly annoy you (why didn't they start further back if they're going to run that fast?). So do the people running quickly (why are they taking it all so seriously and who the absolute heck do they think they are, anyway?).

All of this puts you into an automatic gear, when you won't think about the exertion you are putting your body into. Instead, you will just run like the clappers without a second thought.

Harvard Medical School research found that the sympathetic nervous system sends messages to the adrenal glands at this stage. Adrenaline pours into the bloodstream and endorphins are released. Meanwhile, your heart beats faster and blood rushes to the muscles, allowing them to work harder with no perceived uptake in effort.

So you'll be out there again this Saturday, furiously running along, unable to believe the behaviour of everyone around you. All this huffing and puffing as you work up a sweat – are you sure you shouldn't be a cyclist? (Joke, obviously!)

Remember...

You *can* buy your own timing chip, but everyone will think you are a bit weird.

Running Wisdom

While running can help ease unpleasant emotional states, the reverse can also be true, as a 2015 study called 'Adversity and Superior Olympic Performance' found. Interviewing 10 Olympic gold medallists, researchers from Nottingham Trent University's Open Access Institutional Repository found that all 10 had experienced trauma in their lives. All 10 also believed that the traumatic experiences had positively influenced their results due to the added motivation it gave them to succeed.

Funny Spectator Signs at Running Events

Hurry and you can STILL make it to MASS.

Funny Spectator Signs at Running Events

Did you Know?

The College of Podiatry found that 10 per cent of respondents had to be treated by their family doctor because of injuries caused by badly fitting training shoes. The same study found that 19 per cent of those who buy trainers in physical stores do not get a proper fitting before handing over their cash, while 33 per cent buy their shoes online, and therefore do not try them on at all before purchase.

Runners You Know:
The Running Club Recruiter

A member of a neighbouring running club, you proselytise its wonders with marathon-like persistence. Even Jehovah's Witnesses could learn from you.

Remember...

Don't do anything new the day of a race. That means don't eat or drink anything unfamiliar, don't try any new stretches, don't wear any new running clothing (particularly footwear), or, indeed, do anything new. Race day is not the day to try new things. Got it?

My Running Story:
Olympic Medallist Liz Yelling

Sometimes life can tangle up your thoughts. At times like that I find there is nothing better than going out for a run. It really untangles and irons everything out. You come back refreshed and clarified.

Even when I'm not training, I realise that I still need running in my life. It would be easy, once you've ceased to be an elite athlete, not to run any more, or at least to run a lot less frequently. But for me, I find that I don't feel normal without running in my life. It just makes me more level headed and gives me greater perspective on everything. That makes me a nicer person to be around. I used to get the grumps sometimes if injury stopped me from running. I think most of us do – we feel annoyed when an injury stops us from pursuing our goals.

Nowadays, it isn't injuries that threaten to stop me from running, it's more my duties as a busy mum and just life in general. So I have to regularly remind myself that as soon as I get out there, I can reset my mental haziness. Ultimately, that's a benefit for everyone in my life, not just me.

Running gives me the time and space to process thoughts and the chance to make plans I can act on at a later date. When I run I feel like I can cope with anything that life throws at me. I take things on the chin much more. I'm more mentally prepared to be strong.

When emotions get on top of you, just one little thing can topple you over. But if you've been for a run, you can withstand a lot more because it helps you to use all your emotions in the right way.

I think this is so important with children. You don't want to get things wrong with kids, you don't want to scream and shout at them, but sometimes it is hard to remain calm.

As a parent you obviously have a real pull to be with the children all the time, that sense of responsibility. It's almost like you have a tether to your kids. But going for a run, and stretching that tether, gives you head space, which helps you do the right thing by your family.

Any females who want to start running, or do more running, could consider entering a women-only race – events that help women take their first steps into running with more confidence and in a less scary environment.

The thing is that when women (and I'm sure some men) first start running they can feel very self-conscious – about their shape or even about the very concept of running making them look silly. These anxieties can become stronger in front of men. I'm not saying men want to make women feel self-conscious, but that's sometimes how they end up feeling, and women-only races remove this aspect.

Once people start, they realise it's great to get out there and start moving. Running is one of the only things in life that you nearly always feel better for having done. Even on the odd occasion when you have a bad run there are things you can take from it. You've still been out in the open air being active over however many miles and will feel mentally refreshed and so much the better for it.

That's very much the case for me. I live in Dorset, England, and there are so many beautiful places to run: we have 13 kilometres (8 miles) of prom, and lots of moorland and heath. We are lucky enough to live in a lovely environment and I feel very motivated to get out there. There's a really active outdoor environment that helps people get outside and move.

I rarely wear headphones when I run – I prefer to hear the sound of nature: the chirp of the birds, the sound of the wind and the sea. I feel grounded to the earth through my senses and away with the fairies with my thoughts. Hearing what is going on around me is a big part of that. I love seeing how nature changes day by day and week by week. That in itself is exhilarating.

I think some people really underestimate the power of exercise and the close proximity of physical health with mental health. There's a very strong connection there. I don't just run for physical health, I run for emotional well-being as well. I think the two are inextricably linked.

So I will always be a big advocate for encouraging people to move, to be active. Just get outside, even if it's only for a walk, or to take part in any other sport. Although running is my bag, I'm very in favour of getting people going so they can enjoy the benefits exercise brings.

Speaking of which, I think I'll stop writing this now. I'm going to put on my running shoes and untangle some thoughts...

Liz is a double Olympian and Commonwealth medallist, a world-class marathoner and a highly respected female coach. She has set the women's course record for Bath Half Marathon and Reading Half Marathon. She is a wife and a mum to a beautiful girl and twin boys.

Things We Hate About Running: Uncooperative Communicators

Any conversation that doesn't give me the chance to mention I've run three marathons is simply unacceptable. It's almost like these people aren't interested. What's their problem?

Remember...

You should generally include at least one 32-kilometre (20-mile) training run before a marathon. I cringe when first-timers tell me they plan to run a marathon having done nothing longer than, say, 24 kilometres (15 miles) during training. Going to 32 kilometres (20 miles) or beyond not only gives you a host of physical benefits, but it also offers a psychological boost: knowing that you can run 32 kilometres (20 miles) makes it far less intimidating mentally to approach 42.16 kilometres (26.2 miles) on the big day.

Sure, it's hard and long but since when has that been a bad thing?

Funny Spectator Signs at Running Events

Ooh, You Rotten Cheat!

Cheating in races is nothing new, but it remains and always has been something that just isn't sportsmanlike.

Among some of the more notorious cheats is Spyridon Belokas, who at the 1896 Olympics was one of 17 athletes to start the marathon race. He went on to finish third, but it was later discovered that he had covered part of the course of the race by carriage rather than on foot and he was therefore disqualified.

All was not as it seemed either when Fred Lorz won the men's marathon in the 1904 St Louis Olympics nearly 15 minutes ahead of his nearest rival. Looking jubilant, the 'victor' went on to have his photograph taken with Alice Roosevelt, the daughter of the President.

In fact, Lorz had withdrawn from the race after running 14.5 kilometres (9 miles) and had been driven by his coach for 17.7 kilometres (11 miles). The car had then broken down, so Lorz had hopped out and continued on foot for the rest of course. When he reached the finishing line, blissfully unaware spectators greeted him as the winner, and instead of explaining the situation, he had gone along with it.

When it was discovered what had happened, Lorz's medal was handed to Thomas Hicks. However, it later emerged that he too had been helped on his way, aided by a cocktail of strychnine sulfate (a common rat poison) and brandy – a mixture that was banned in subsequent years.

The controversy continued in the 1908 London Olympics marathon event when the wonderfully monikered Dorando Pietri finished first, but was subsequently disqualified. This time, however, the problem was not that the runner had hitched a ride. Instead, the issue lay with the fact that in the final mile, Pietri, who had become exhausted and dehydrated, in a state of bewilderment had taken the wrong path and required umpires to redirect him. He then fell down five times, and was helped up and along by the umpires each time.

He eventually finished the race in first place – despite it taking him 10 minutes to complete the final 350 metres (350 yards) – but the American team, one of whom finished second, filed a complaint about the help Pietri had received from the umpires. The Italian was subsequently disqualified and removed from the final standings of the race.

Despite this stripping of laurels, all was not doom and gloom. Pietri might have lost the battle (the marathon) but he won the war (the hearts of the public); after Queen Alexandra gave him a gilded silver cup, he went on to become an international celebrity, and composer Irving Berlin even dedicated a song to him entitled 'Dorando'.

Fame of a less favourable nature came to New Yorker Rosie Ruiz some 70 years later when she was busted in 1979 for cheating at the New York City Marathon. She had been spotted leaving the course after only 16 kilometres (10 miles), taking the subway train to Columbus Circle, and then walking to the finish. Having clearly not learned her lesson, she was also accused of cheating at the Boston Marathon just five months later, and was stripped of her winner's medal when it emerged that she had taken the subway from Cambridge to Boston, re-joined the course and run to the finish line.

More recently, food blogger Jane Seo was stripped of second place in the Fort Lauderdale Half Marathon after it was claimed she had found a shortcut that shaved about 2.3 kilometres (1.4 miles) off her run. This time it was not witnesses but her running tech coupled with advanced photographic equipment that exposed the cheating. The skulduggery came to light when an eagle-eyed independent marathon investigator called Derek Murphy zoomed in on a photo of the Harvard graduate posing after the race, and noted that her fitness tracker recorded a distance of just 18.75 kilometres (11.65 miles).

She later admitted the offence in an Instagram post, writing of her 'HORRIBLE' choice to 'CUT THE COURSE'. Switching off her caps-lock key she added: 'I cheated and should have disqualified myself.'

The moral of all these stories, folks, is DON'T CHEAT!

Things We Hate About Running: Garbage Trucks

Many an early morning has been destroyed by running past one of these as they go about their business. With your lungs open and your body taking deep, deep breaths, the fumes of rancid alcohol and general decaying rubbish are the last things you want to take in on your dawn trot.

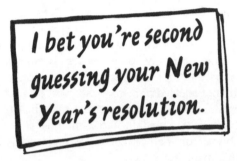

I bet you're second guessing your New Year's resolution.

Funny Spectator Signs at Running Events

Runners You Know: 45-Degree Man

Usually an elderly short man, the 45-degree runner leans forwards dramatically as they run. By the end of a half marathon they are practically horizontal. Each of us has different running gaits but these are exceptional.

It is always annoying, as you run along with your perfect gait, when a 45-degree runner twice your age powers past you. That's the trouble with the elderly, no respect. [See also: 'The Inexplicably Good Old Runner' on page 13.]

My Running Story: US Olympian and Running Coach Jeff Galloway

At the age of 13, I was a very overweight, lazy kid. I wasn't proud of being fat, and realised that exercise could be a key to losing my extra baggage, but in my internal priority list, far ahead of being lean was the avoidance of exercise. I now know that I had programmed myself to believe that it hurt because of some puking incidents due to being pushed too hard by a PE coach who wanted to help me get in shape.

As I began my 8th-grade year, I enrolled in a school that required male students to engage in strenuous activities or sports after school. The head coach was the most lenient in the place, and allowed us 'options'. I initially joined a group of lazy kids who would jog 200 metres (200 yards) to the woods and goof off.

But one day an older kid who I liked said, 'Galloway, you're running with us today.' My anxiety soared because these kids actually ran long distances – 3 whole miles! I had my lazy-boy strategy in place: when I reached the protective cover of the woods I would grab my leg, claim I was injured, and throw rocks in the creek as they ran on. But then the runners started telling jokes, and then began to gossip about other students. I listened at first, huffing and puffing. Even when I was physically exhausted after most of these runs, I felt better in my brain and my spirit than ever before. With a little more fitness I began to participate in the conversations. We shared stories, argued, and more than anything else, enjoyed the fun environment that we created each day.

After a few months I found myself hooked on the endorphin experience. My grades significantly improved. I discovered that even when things had not been going well at school or 'in life', a run of 20 minutes or more turned my attitude around. The bonding resulted in honest friendships based upon mutual respect. I'm still enjoying these benefits over half a century later.

But there was something more powerful about the running experience that pulled me out on the roads and trails by myself when the school year ended. Regardless of how tired or stressed I felt before, I received a boost to mind, body and spirit afterwards, which was life-changing.

After analysing the research on the benefits to the brain of various exercises, for my book *Mental Training*, I discovered that running turns on brain circuits for a better attitude, greater vitality, and personal empowerment more effectively than any other activity studied. These circuits stimulate hormones that change the brain in many positive ways. The bottom line is that after a run we feel better about ourselves and about the quality of life. This explains the positive benefits that I had experienced from my first runs.

Research on critical thinking has revealed significant benefits for those who run for 45 minutes or more regularly (running non-stop is not required):

- New brain cell growth at any age;
- Quicker problem-solving;
- Better decisions;
- Quicker learning;
- Better memory.

Many are drawn to running because of these powerful and unique rewards. Without the right tools, however, some runners push too hard, and break something, burn out, or even puke as I did. A common misconception is that they are not designed to run. Actually, most of us inherited all of the adaptations required for running.

In digging deeper into motivation for example, I discovered that there are two brain 'operating systems' that we use in conducting the behaviours we choose to perform. The ancient subconscious 'monkey brain' has 1 million times the processing capability of our human conscious brain. When we start an activity we have done repeatedly, such as running, we tend to let the ancient brain take over. This is usually fine at first, but as the stress builds up due to exertion, heat, time constraints, goals, etc, the 'monkey' will secrete anxiety hormones and then negative hormones that reduce motivation and make us miserable.

You don't have to eliminate the stress to stop the negative hormones. By having cognitive strategies the human brain takes control, overrides the 'monkey' and stops the hormones. This puts you in charge in terms of your attitude and the challenges that pop up during a run.

I've discovered that for each challenge there is a cognitive strategy that can allow us to take charge of our running, reducing injury risk and boosting motivation. A new world opens up as we become the captains of our ships, navigating the challenges, experiencing the empowerment and learning along the way.

Jeff Galloway is an Olympian runner who now works as a coach. He has trained more than 200,000 people, and is also an author and a columnist for Runners World. *www.jeffgalloway.com*

Things People Shout at Runners

Did you Know?

About 86.7 million – the number of runs uploaded to the Strava app in 2016, logging a total running distance of 718.6 million kilometres (446.5 million miles) – the equivalent of over 900 return trips to the moon.

Running Philosophy

❝ Pain is inevitable. Suffering is optional. Say you're running and you think, 'Man, this hurts, I can't take it anymore.' The 'hurt' part is an unavoidable reality, but whether or not you can stand anymore is up to the runner himself. **❞**

Haruki Murakami, author

Why Getting Fit is Like Getting High

There you are, sprawled out on the sofa, exhausted but feeling wonderfully tranquil and reassured – everything in the world seems to have a warm glow about it.

You're also ravenously hungry, and you just know that anything you eat or drink will taste divine. But at the same time you are not sure you can muster the co-ordination to walk to the kitchen and find sustenance. Instead, you might have a little nap.

Question: have you just a) run a half marathon, or b) smoked pot?

Even if in your case the answer is 'a', it could just as easily be 'b'. Long runs and long smokes have for years been said to bestow similar effects – and now scientists have discovered why.

A 2016 study at the University of Oxford concluded that the post-run buzz could be sparked not by endorphins, which were previously thought to cause the high, but by substances called cannabinoids. Yes, the same stuff that's found in marijuana.

By common lore, runners and stoners seem radically different to one another, almost separate species – the former all smug, healthy and active, the latter shy, wheezy and lazy.

Yet they have much in common. Members of both groups are, generally, comfortable in solitude, and willing to go through pain barriers of various kinds to achieve that warm glow, which strips away anxiety and glues you to your chair. Both toking and running also work up an appetite, and in particular a craving for carbs.

Dedicated caners and runners vehemently insist that their respective activity is not addictive – yet both pastimes continue to attract the suspicion that they are a 'gateway drug' on the path to harder stuff (higher-class substances and ultramarathons respectively).

In truth, the insistence that smoking and running are not addictive is contradicted by the anxious, self-pitying sulk that pursuers of both activities fall into if their hobby of choice is denied them by, say, a lack of supply or a niggly knee injury.

The link isn't just theoretical. A growing number of ultramarathon runners are now turning to pot as a training aid. Cannabis can block pain, fend off nausea and lessen boredom, thus taking out three of the greatest enemies of those who take part in epic runs, which can be as long as 320 kilometres (200 miles) and are often competed over hellish terrain.

In recognition and partial acceptance of this trend, the World Anti-Doping Agency (WADA) has raised the permitted level of one of cannabis' active ingredients, THC, from its previous threshold of 15 nanograms per millilitre to 150 nanograms per millilitre. Athletes are now allowed, in effect, to use the drug in training and even the night before a race, but not during the event itself, where its use would be regarded as violating the spirit of the sport.

As the worlds of potheads and runners grow ever closer, a company called 420 Games has been formed in California (where else?). Named after the dope-smokers' slang term that signifies the time of day at which many like to spark up, 420 Games aims to 'show that cannabis users are not lazy, unmotivated or stoners', hoping that 'via athletic achievement we will change the stereotypes built up during the era of prohibition'.

Earlier this year, the group organised a 6.8 kilometre (4.2 mile) run in San Francisco, with the tag line 'everything in moderation except sweat'. As part of the post-run entertainment, reggae artist Pato Banton performed.

The stereotype that pot smokers lack ambition or competitiveness is being dented. Athlete and advocate Chris Barnicle claims to be 'the world's fastest stoner'. The worlds are also colliding altruistically. The Marijuana Marathon Man runs events to raise support and awareness for medicinal marijuana treatment. With more states and countries decriminalising cannabis, all this might be a trend to watch.

Before we get carried away, though, we should remember that cannabis increases heart rate, can accelerate muscle fatigue and bring on cardiovascular disease and, when smoked, damage your lungs. None of this is ideal for running. Then there are the potential emotional effects: a fit of hysterical giggling or bout of swivel-eyed paranoia are unlikely to do you many favours mid-way through a 10k.

Many runners swear on a quick puff as a post-run ritual, as much for its anti-inflammatory as its psychological effects. But for many of us, the natural high that runs give us more than suffices in their aftermath.

This natural high is what running is all about. For us, the shedding of calories and toning of body are secondary benefits; the joy is in how good a run makes us feel, how it leaves us glowing.

So, fellow runners, try not to look down upon those who choose to get high on the sofa rather than in the park. We're both chasing the same compounds.

Funny Spectator Signs at Running Events

Running Myths Reconsidered: Caffeine Will Dehydrate You

While studies show that the caffeine equivalent of two cups of coffee will slightly increase your urine output for up to three hours, research also shows that exercise cancels out that side effect. Caffeine has also been shown to improve performance.

Notable Runners: Dean Karnazes

This man's running biography is exhausting just to read. In 2005, he ran 563 kilometres (350 miles) without sleeping. It took him 80 hours and 44 minutes. The following year, he ran in 50 marathons in 50 US states over 50 consecutive days.

Remember...

It's best to wait for around two hours after a meal before running. Some people say they can run just 90 minutes after eating, others go as low as 60 or even 45 minutes. But really, is it worth the risk? Head out too soon and your grub may not be properly digested, which intensifies the risks of abdominal cramps, bloating and spewing. Not nice.

Did you Know?

Around 509,000 Americans completed a marathon in 2015.

My Running Story: Hypnotherapist and Author Lisa Jackson

For me, running is like tea. It's something I simply can't live without, and has the seemingly miraculous ability to calm me down, gee me up and provide solace on the darkest days. When I was retraining as a hypnotherapist and studying for five hours a day in addition to doing a demanding day job, it was running that proved a sanity saver: pounding the pavements three times a week was my self-created version of Valium. When I've lacked motivation while writing my three books it's been running-induced perspiration that's provided my inspiration. When I needed comforting after my beloved mother was killed by a reckless driver while out training for a marathon, I turned to running to heal my heart.

When I'm drinking tea, I've consciously uncoupled myself from the relentless pester power of unanswered emails; I'm no longer checking my phone to see if I've missed a client's call. All that matters in that moment is feeling the warmth of that steaming 'hug in a mug' – and taking time to sit and stare. And if it's a pleasure shared with friends and family, so much the better.

Running is just the same, except that it involves an endlessly fascinating change of scenery and, of course, the chance to chat to a never-ending array of extraordinary runners. People such as Dawn, who lost her sister to cancer and channelled her grief into raising thousands of pounds for charity by running marathons in outrageous fancy dress. Or 81-year-old Robbie, who beat me in one of the hardest and hilliest marathons I've ever run. Or Paul, who's now done 312 marathons and hasn't let being blind since the age of six stop him from living his dreams.

Running is the most life-affirming activity I know. Yes, for me, it's most definitely my cup of tea.

Clinical hypnotherapist Lisa Jackson (www.quiet-medicine.co.uk) is the author of Your Pace or Mine? *(Summersdale, 2016),* Running Made Easy *(Pavilion, 2014) and* Adore Yourself Slim *(Simon & Schuster, 2011).*

Runners You Know: The Serial Stretcher

Wherever you are, whatever you're doing, you stretch. You probably do graveside lunges at family funerals.

Running Philosophy

❝ I always loved running ... it was something you could do by yourself, and under your own power. You could go in any direction, fast or slow as you wanted, fighting the wind if you felt like it, seeking out new sights just on the strength of your feet and the courage of your lungs. **❞**

Jesse Owens, four-time Olympic gold medallist

Remember...

Never increase your weekly mileage by more than 10 per cent each week. This is widely accepted wisdom.

You're hot and have stamina (call me).

Funny Spectator Signs at Running Events

The A–Z of Vegetarian Running Food

Plenty of books, magazines and websites will give you tips on which meats to consume to help you with running and other exercises. Here, let's take a look at the veggie options...

Almonds

Eating nuts lowers circulating artery-clogging cholesterol levels, reducing your risk of heart disease. They also address inflammation.

Amaranth

Do you find yourself awake at night wondering which grain offers more protein than quinoa? Of course you do. Well, amaranth is that grain.

Avocado

These pears are rich in vitamin E, which reduces inflammation.

Bananas

There's a reason why at any serious running event you will see people clutching bunches of this fruit. It's an energy booster packed with carbs, and also has lashing of potassium, which regulates blood pressure and reduces your risk of stroke.

Broccoli

If you want vitamin C, potassium, fibre and phytochemicals, then you cannot do better than eating some of this green. All of those are key for peak performance and health. If you really are not a fan of broccoli, then you can try blending it. Either way, it is well worth learning to love it – you will be repaid richly.

Cherries

These fruits are rich with antioxidants called anthocyanins, which boost performance in running and other sports. A study showed that rowers suffered less strength loss and soreness after cherry juice was added to their diet.

Dark chocolate

The potent antioxidants in chocolate can boost heart health. They also ease inflammation and lower the risk of potential blood clots. So what are you waiting for? Get some dark chocolate down your gullet!

Dried dates

A quick source of carbs, they are also full of potassium, which helps your muscles to function.

Edamame

These green soybeans are popular in Japan and, increasingly, elsewhere. They are a rich source of protein.

Flaxseed

Sprinkled into smoothies or on top of porridge, these whole or ground seeds are a great way of getting omega-3 essential fats without eating fish.

Ginger

Have some every day to avoid post-run aches and pains.

Honey

Sugar is digested quickly, causing spikes in blood-glucose levels. Honey is a sweet way of getting more stable energy.

Incaberries

These have a higher antioxidant capacity than many fruits, plus plenty of protein, potassium and phosphorus. What more do you want?

Juice

So long as you avoid overly sugary concentrated ones made solely from fruit, juices can be a brilliant way to boost your daily intake of fruit and vegetables and top up your nutrient levels. Cherry juice and beetroot or beet juice are thought to be especially beneficial for runners, but ones made with a rainbow of different fresh ingredients will all be beneficial.

Kale

This leafy food has become the butt of many jokes about vegans, dinner-partying liberals, and other groups. A member of the cabbage clan, it is rich in a number of vitamins and minerals that are useful for running, including vitamins A, B6, C and K. Particularly pertinent for runners is that it has useful anti-inflammatory properties. So crunch on some kale and knock down your chances of tightness and injury.

Leeks

These versatile alliums are rich in kaempferol, a flavonoid that protects blood vessel linings from damage. While you are running, this will help your body get all the oxygen it needs. Leeks also contain folate, a B vitamin that protects against cardiovascular diseases.

Mushrooms

They might not scream healthy when you look at them but mushrooms are bursting with nutrients that help runners generate energy and repair cells. Among these are vitamins B and D.

Nuts

Many a runner is nuts about nuts – and with good reason. Monounsaturated fat delays the onset of muscle fatigue, and electrolytes prevent cramp.

Oranges

A study from the University of North Carolina at Greensboro found that taking vitamin C supplements for two weeks prior to challenging exercise helped alleviate muscle soreness. Oranges supply over 100 per cent of the Daily Value (DV) for the antioxidant vitamin C, and are therefore essential for runners. They can lower cholesterol and blood pressure, too.

Peanut butter

Spread a generous amount of this over a bagel and you have a running superfood right there in front of you. It will give you carbs and protein, and prove surprisingly easy to digest. A true runners' staple.

Quinoa

This grain has become something of a laughing stock – the clichéd staple of the liberal-leaning cook's kitchen. For runners, though, it provides plenty of nutrients, including iron and carbs. So, ignore those who scoff at its associations and get stuck in.

Rice

Try it brown – it has the same amount of carbs as white rice but it provides a slower-burning energy and is higher in fibre.

Soy

Soy lowers cholesterol and helps prevent osteoporosis. Researchers at Ohio State University also found that soy protein is as effective as whey protein in promoting muscle growth after training. Music to the ears of vegan runners, including your author!

Sweet potatoes

Manganese and copper are important minerals for runners because they are vital for healthy muscle function. Sadly, many runners are short on both. The answer is sweet potatoes, which are a rich source, and also provide vitamin A, vitamin C, potassium and iron. Moreover, they both taste and look far more interesting than your average spud.

Turmeric

This spice includes a compound called curcumin – a powerful antioxidant that also decreases inflammation. Add more to your diet and wave goodbye to stiffness, sore limbs and aching joints. It also has all manner of generally useful properties, including the enhancement of your heart's health.

Umeboshi

These pickled plums – sometimes known as Japanese apricots – could become the next big thing for the savvy running community since they fend off exhaustion by converting stored lactic acid into water and carbon dioxide.

Vegetable soup

Simple and good, always best when made at home using seasonal vegetables.

Watermelon

A rich source of vitamin C, which helps maintain joint flexibility, watermelons are also hugely refreshing after a long run. As a bonus, they will help protect your skin from pollution, UV rays and sweat.

Xmas dinner (meat free)

Because even the most nutritionally-obsessed, rice-weighing runners can afford to take at least one day off their careful, measured eating. (And I needed an 'X'...)

Yellow pawpaw

These exotic fruits include vitamins A, C, E and K, folate, potassium, and a range of antioxidants. Yum.

Ziti

Whatever event you are carb-loading for, you can use this tubular pasta to help you through the challenge. Particularly if the challenge is completing an A–Z...

Funny Spectator Signs at Running Events

Runners You Know: The Sudden Stopper

As you finish a long running event, you can feel so climactic while you cross the line that it is easy to lose yourself. The sudden stoppers find it very easy to lose themselves.

These are the runners who, the moment they pass the finishing line, stop dead and stand there, basking in the glory of it all. Which is kind of sweet, but also kind of annoying, particularly for other runners who either have to dodge these sudden stoppers or risk some sort of perspiring pile-up, right when they want one the least.

So please, runners, keep moving at the end, or at least move to the side.

Weird Marathons: Everest Marathon

With most marathons it is a struggle to get to the finish, but with this one it is also a challenge to reach the starting line. To acclimatise to the high altitude, participants hike for 15 days before race day. Then they set off, at 6.30 a.m. on a route that includes snow, ice, yaks and perilously narrow suspension bridges. Along with the usual marathon hazards, this one chucks in a host of other risks, such as altitude sickness and hypothermia.

Notable Runners: Budhia Singh

A boy from the slums of India, Singh tackled his first marathon at the tender age of three. By the time he was four, he had run 48 marathons. Later, a film was made about him, entitled *Budhia Singh: Born to Run*.

Who's chasing you?

Things People Shout at Runners

Things We Hate About Running:
Litter bugs

Runners who drop their bottle/cup/gel wrapper on the middle of the course are a serious menace. When the area around a drinks station is wet and strewn with various plastic and foil detritus, the chances of a runner slipping over and breaking something are horribly high. Seriously, people, either use one of the bins or at least throw your waste as far off the course as you can.

Running Wisdom

❝ Every major decision I've made in the last eight years has been prefaced by a run. ❞

Casey Neistat, filmmaker

Things We Hate About Running:
The Runner's Build

People who aren't at all athletic sometimes imagine that pounding the pavement gives men the build of a fitness-mag cover star, and women a similarly coveted physique.

In fact, running is more likely to leave men looking like the puny geek of every American frat movie and is liable to reduce the bust size of committed female runners to that of a pre-teen. It is a one-dimensional activity that exercises specific muscles but leaves the others unaffected. So, while it can build impressive legs, it often gives the runner a puny chest. All of this looks good enough with your clothes on, but as they come off, the spectacle can become a little nightmarish.

The Joy of Escape

In wilder eras of human history running was often used as a method of escape – from enemies on the battlefield, from predatory wild animals, and more. More recently, people have sprinted from crime scenes, dashed for a bus or trotted for a train. If you want to escape or catch something, running is a great thing.

Running can also indirectly give you an out from tedious or stressful situations. It is an ever-present excuse that you can keep under your running belt, ready to whip out when you feel trapped by some sort of ghastly situation.

Here are some such scenarios:

Family Christmases

Homes can become cramped over the festive season as relatives descend to spend a hellish amount of time over-eating, supping mulled wine and generally getting on one another's nerves. Board games are played, small talk is exchanged and farts are emitted.

It's hard to escape this familial claustrophobia. If you suggest going to the pub, at least half the relatives will act as if you've murdered a small child. If you announce you are going on a walk, some Christmas jumper-clad bore will come with you, meaning you haven't escaped the problem but merely moved it elsewhere.

However, provided you are the only runner in the clan, you can find a ready-made excuse to get the hell out of there for a few hours. Heck, even if there are other runners in the flock who want to join you, you can just put your foot down and leave them in your wake, or at least get them so breathless that you render the bores speechless.

The feeling of freedom that an open-air run brings you will be a welcome contrast to the sedentary confinement of the house. You might even find you enjoy yourself for a tiny bit of Christmas – and that's no mean feat.

Unwanted social invitations

The trick here is to keep your running schedule as secret as possible. That way, when you are invited to some sort of bash that sounds like social hell, you can merely say that you've a long training run or special event to attend the following morning.

This excuse is best deployed as a way to leave functions early, rather than to avoid them altogether. Turn up, ostentatiously decline to drink alcohol and then announce that you'll have to leave soon, using the aforementioned running excuse.

It's a fairly solid pretext – and anyway, no party is ever sad to see the back of a tee-totaller.

Ghastly food

Maybe you're at a dinner party or perhaps you're simply visiting your parents for a bit of grub. Either way, it can be generally hard to decline any offers of seconds, even when the food is borderline inedible.

However, when you are a runner you have a ready-made excuse to eat only as much as you want of everything. Indeed, this manoeuvre works just as well in reverse – so should you want to pull rank on your fellow diners and chow down on more than your fair share of food, just say you're loading up for a run.

Use injury complaints

Claiming you are crocked opens up a vast range of things to dodge: parties, DIY duties, and much more besides. So practice your best faux limp.

Run now, TEQUILA later.

Funny Spectator Signs at Running Events

Remember...

If you are wondering whether your shorts are too short, or, for men, if it is a problem that the inner lining has perished, then the answer to both questions is almost certainly an urgent 'yes'. Get ye to a running store.

Did you Know?

A distance of 19.3 kilometres (12 miles) a day for 2075 days is what you would have to run to complete 400,000 kilometres (24,900 miles) – the circumference of the planet.

Running Wisdom

The Jewish philosopher Hillel was once asked if he could sum up the entire Torah, the central reference of Judaism, while standing on one leg. Hillel replied: 'That which is hateful unto you do not do to your neighbour. This is the whole of the Torah. The rest is commentary. Now go and study.'

If I had to sum up everything I want to say about running while standing on one leg, I would say: 'Listen to your body and have fun – the rest is commentary.' Now go and run...

My Running Story:
Comedian and Author David Baddiel

People who like running say: 'It's meditative: I get to think about so many things while I run. The air, the birds, nature, my life...' I think about one thing: running. How much it hurts, and how soon it's going to stop.

Which is why I don't run any more. I used to. I ran to lose weight – although that would not seem to be working, seeing as my weight has remained on a steady upward trajectory since 1994 – and I ran to pay lip service to the idea of keeping fit, but, much more, I ran because it is the only thing that really works for depression. Which I was, in my 30s: depressed.

There is a typical irony in this, in that the major symptom of depression is stasis: depression means exactly that, to be 'pressed down', and therefore not to want to move. Instead you just feel you have to sit or lie with that weight – in bed, or on a chair, or on the floor. Running's role in combating depression is – just – worth the depression induced by the idea of running.

I came to this conclusion after many years of combining therapy with antidepressants. I tried every antidepressant on the market. Of the standard selective serotonin reuptake inhibitors (SSRIs), Prozac made me woozy and insomniac; Paroxetine made me more anxious than before; Citalopram had no effect; and Zoloft made me fat. All of them made me anorgasmic.

So I ran. And it did work. Five minutes into a run, I could feel the moment when depression lifts – or rather, when it bursts. It's a painful release, similar to that experienced when dabbing medicated gel on mouth ulcers, like the pain has to maximise before it will go away. I felt the depression in combination, all of its physical symptoms – hot flushes, pins and needles, anxiety shoots in the stomach – coming together as one before they dissipated, like when dying people revive for one last time before they vanish.

This dissipation is temporary – the depression comes back – but it's a massive relief for a short time. Oh, and by the way, it took me a while to realise that the responsibility for this relief lay with running. I remember sitting in a hot tub at my local gym after 25 minutes on the treadmill and thinking, almost in tears, God, Paroxetine really works.

David Baddiel is one of Britain's most distinguished comedians, the star of The Mary Whitehouse Experience, Fantasy Football League *and* Baddiel and Skinner Unplanned. *He has also written seven books, a movie and a play.*

Funny Spectator Signs at Running Events

Remember...

When you are just 5 kilometres (3 miles) away from the end of a half marathon or marathon, that distance can seem ridiculously long. So, a good trick is to imagine the same distance at home. Imagine where you'd be if you were that distance from your home. Begin to mentally picture the various landmarks you would pass, the turns, the street markers. It works!

Remember...

When weather conditions are bad for a running event, simply reminding yourself that they are bad for everyone there can help you plough on. Realising the conditions are not a personal attack on you seems to make all the difference.

Did you Know?

Three days' travelling at 24km/h (15mph) – the amount of non-stop running that the average man's energy level would support.

Runners You Know:
The Ultramarathon Junkie

Some people say running is as addictive as various naughty substances – and the ultramarathon junkie is living proof of this. For these folk, the 10ks and half marathons that satisfy most runners are merely gateway experiences into the class-A thrills of the ultramarathon.

With distances ranging from 50–100 kilometres (31–62 miles), ultramarathons seem like mammoth undertakings to the outsider. Perhaps a once-in-a-lifetime challenge for a runner, or at the very most an annual affair. But the ultramarathon junkie just can't get enough.

Before they know it, they are taking on double marathons, 24-hour races and even multi-day events. When their bolstered tolerance levels drain the challenge out of any distance, the runners simply attempt it on a more testing terrain: muddy surfaces, mountainous humps or even roasting deserts. They are out there all weekend, every weekend.

In fact, life for these runners consists almost entirely of three things: running, filling in entry forms for running events, and sleeping. They have a year-round cold and a haunted look in their eyes. Because their bodies ache all the time, they long ago lost track of whether they are injured or merely knackered. They're also hungry all the time.

But what thrills there are to be had. The excitement of signing up, the enormous sense of achievement that you feel as you stumble over the finishing line having run 100 kilometres (62 miles). Your body is ruined, you've trained so long and hard that you can hardly remember what your family and friends look like – but you did it!

From the Stopwatch to Strava: A Timeline of Running Gadgets and Technology

Stopwatch

Controversy reigns over the question of who first invented the stopwatch. The first historical evidence of the gadget came in 1776, when Frenchmen Jean-Moyes Pouzai produced a very basic one under the name 'Chronograph'. Later, an Englishman called George Graham created a device that could start and stop at a speed as fast as 1/16th of a second, and it all evolved from thereon in, going digital in the 1970s. As a gizmo it brings a certain gravitas to its bearer – as you hold it, timing the activity of someone else, how can you not feel like some sort of masterful coach?

Pedometer

Conceptualised by Leonardo da Vinci, the first pedometer was created in 1780, just four years after the first stopwatch. These were clearly fine times for running tech. Thomas Jefferson later introduced a mechanical pedometer, before more modern versions emerged from Japan in the 1960s.

These early pedometers counted each step a person took by detecting the motion of the user's hands or hips and needed to be configured before use. As a result, there were question marks over how accurate they were. Today, pedometers are a little more accurate and seem to be everywhere, from wrist watch-style activity trackers to your smartphone in your pocket.

The computer shoe

In 1984, adidas launched a running shoe that featured a built-in computer – the Micropacer. The trainers, which were astronaut-metallic in colour, had an electronic pedometer sewn into the tongue, and the shoe's mini computer calculated distance, average pace and calories burned. However, they never really took off, since some runners complained that the shoes were too heavy and others balked at the price tag – 'No person, however rich, should pay $100 for a pair of running shoes,' complained *International Magazine*. The sportswear giant discontinued the shoe in 1987, but re-released it in 2014.

GPS

The Garmin Forerunner was launched in 2003, leading to a revolution in running gadgetry. However, GPS – the technology it relies on – dates back to several decades earlier, when the Soviet Union launched the first man-made satellite, *Sputnik 1*, in 1957, and paved the way for future satellites to be launched into space. Physicists went on to realise that they could pinpoint exactly where the satellite was along its orbit, and the concept of GPS was born. One small (OK, fairly major!) step for satellites, one giant leap for the running community.

Strava

In 2009, running joined the social networking revolution with the launch of Strava, a website and mobile app that is used to track your miles via GPS. If you are obsessed with data then this is the thing for you. It can also play to your competitive and nosy side because you can peruse the progress of other runners.

Nike FuelBand

This activity tracker was launched in 2012. Designed to be used with the iPhone, iPad or Android device, it allowed the user to track their physical activity, steps taken daily, and amount of energy burned. By pouring this data into the Nike+ online community, wearers could set goals and compare their progress with that of other runners. However, in 2014 Nike decided to move away from wearable technology and focus more on digital business.

My Money Time

Have you ever dreamed of becoming a professional runner who is paid to do your favourite activity? Well now you can be – in a way. This app tracks your runs by tying in with other apps such as Strava. The further you run, the more money credits you build up. You can then exchange these virtual funds for online discount vouchers for ASICS, adidas and other top brands.

PARA'KITO

A godsend for runners in mosquito-ridden areas, this is a wristband that repels the little rascals. It features a refillable cartridge that will fend them off for 15 days.

Smart running shoes

These shoes, such as the Altra IQ, give you a range of feedback on your running, thanks to the chip that records data such as cadence and foot strike. It will also measure your force of impact and lots more detail of your running form. Too attached to your normal running shoes to consider the change? There are also smart socks.

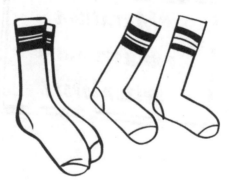

Drones

Some runners take a drone out with them for their morning jog, to film their route. Possibly not one for the average recreational runner.

Notable Runners: Abebe Bikila

In 1960, Bikila became the first Sub-Saharan African to win a gold medal at the Olympics. His achievement was also noteworthy because he ran the marathon barefooted.

Did you Know?

Sixty per cent – the proportion of girls fathered by men who run more than 48 kilometres (30 miles) per week, in a study by the University of Glasgow.

Running Wisdom

" For me, ultra running is 20 per cent physical and 80 per cent mental. *"*

George Anderson, Running coach

Funny Spectator Signs at Running Events

My Running Story: Author Ruth Field

Running has always been therapy for me. When I took it up, it wasn't to lose weight or get fit, but to help balance out my moods while I came off anti-depressants. And the effects were profound. The endorphin rushes thrilled me. After a run I was left feeling spent and capable at the same time. I was astonished how effective running was for lifting my spirits and enabling me in other areas of my life.

There was a period when I was pregnant and for some time after having twins that I was not able to run, and my mental health definitely suffered. When I got back into it again, the impact it had on my well-being and experience as a mother far outweighed all the logistical hurdles of carving out the time and finding the energy for it. I ran because it made me feel like myself again. Since then, I've stuck to it like glue.

For me, a run is the only thing I can do for myself that I know will have a very specific and guaranteed effect on the rest of my day, and in that way it really does work like medicine for me – a powerful vitamin I suppose. If I take my running pill in the morning, I'm going to be more productive at my desk, have more time and patience with my children in the afternoon, approach all my tasks and relationships in a more positive mindset, eat more healthily and sleep more deeply. Any anxiety I have lessens too, so everything feels easier.

This doesn't make it any easier to get out there and go running though! My trick is to try not to think about it as a conscious decision at all, but just to treat it as an essential part of my morning routine: wake up; get dressed for a run; breakfast; take the kids to school carrying nothing but my front-door key; run back home via the woods; sit at my desk and write. Notice I don't shower first. This is only OK because I work alone in the attic. I do shower eventually – just before lunch. This routine works for me. I'm still at my desk by 9.30 a.m. alert, engaged and relaxed, and ready to do my best. But if I miss that slot, which happens more than I'd like, I always find it much harder to motivate myself later on as I can invent a million excuses to trump a run.

The older I get, the more important my runs have become for keeping me fit and healthy, and the more grateful I am that my body can still do it. Long may that privilege continue...

Ruth Field is the author of Run Fat Bitch Run *(Sphere, 2014), a columnist for* The Irish Times, *a motivational speaker and a copywriter. (@GritDoctor)*

Runners You Know: The Proud Marathon Runner

Q: How do you know if someone's run a marathon?
A: They'll tell you.

Things We Hate About Running: Unsolicited Racers

There you are, just about to complete your 5k or 10k happily and at a pace that works for you. Suddenly some puffed-up runner decides to sprint alongside you and then past you, challenging you to a race you neither asked for nor wanted. But, naturally, you find it very hard to resist the challenge. Particularly if you're a middle-aged man.

Running Philosophy

66 Why do we get up extra early, squeeze into lurid apparel and head into a cold morning? Because running is simple and child-like and brilliant. **99**

Vassos Alexander, author of *Don't Stop Me Now*
(Bloomsbury Sport, 2016)

Why Winter Running Rocks

The nights are drawing in, rain is falling more frequently and temperatures are dropping. Ahead, we have the prospect of months of ice, snow and sub-zero conditions. For runners, it must be time to decrease the weekly mileage or even hang up the trainers until spring, right?

Goodness, no. Maybe it's that peculiar masochism that an education at an all-boys school can knock into one, but for me, the harsher the weather, the more I enjoy running.

Ah, it's great out there in the cold. While the fair-weather runners cower indoors, solidarity between us hardier harriers soars. As we pass one another on the pavements and in the parks, we exchange knowing glances that boost our collective vainglory.

Well may we feel delighted with ourselves – running in the cold brings with it objective benefits. First, I'll let you into a secret: running in the cold is actually easier. When temperatures are lower, running inflicts less heat stress on your body, making each step less of an effort.

It has also been suggested (although some dispute it) that runners burn more calories in cold temperatures. So while the rest of you shiver inside, worrying how many calories you're piling on with your festive food, we're out there laughing all the way to the beach body.

Running in the cold is also a fast track to enhanced mental strength. On particularly ghastly days we may emerge into the cold a mouse, but we always return a lion. With every invigorating step we shrug off the seasonal-affective-disorder winter blues.

See it as a battle: the moment you huddle under a rug, winter has beaten you and the only way is down. By getting out there and pounding the pavement you're showing the cold that it messed with the wrong runner.

It's no surprise, then, that while you're out defying sub-zero temperatures, the occupants of every passing car are watching you with what feels like awestruck admiration. It's all they can do to not wind down the window and shout: 'Hey, we can only thank you for showing us what a real hero looks like!'

OK, perhaps I just imagine that. But it's no sillier than some of the things non-runners say to us winter warriors. 'Be careful you don't freeze your lungs,' they offer. Sure, and while we're discussing imaginary medical disasters I'll be careful next summer to not melt my diaphragm or set fire to my face.

'But … what do you do when it rains?' they ask, all concerned and furrowed of brow. Well, I get wet, of course. And what a welcome refresher the rain can be when you're several miles into a decent run. As long as you've got the right gear – and which runner doesn't love an excuse to buy more kit – you'll be fine.

Rain is not the only gift Mother Nature gives runners during the cold months. In autumn she lays a carpet of gold and then in winter she gives us early-rising runners first dibs on striding through a fresh coating of snow. Evening runners, too, benefit from the white stuff: it reflects light, aiding night vision.

It's true, cold winds can be a pain, but when they're at your back they're a helping hand. And trust me, winter sunrises are as breathtaking as a 200m sprint.

It's all so preferable to summer running, when the streets and parks are jammed with human obstacles. Only non-runners think that running on hot, bright days is a treat. Those of us who don our trainers in mid-July know that our heart and sweaty head will thump as we weave around day-tripping families and fair-weather joggers.

No, autumn and winter are the months of the runner. So get out there and get muddy. Little can beat the feeling of coming in from a long, cold, wet run, making yourself a great steaming cup of tea and basking in the satisfaction of it all.

Smug? Absolutely, but better smug than SAD.

Things We Hate About Running: Injuries

Shin splints. Plantar fasciitis. Runner's knee. Achilles tendinitis. Ankle sprain. Iliotibial band syndrome. Lost toenails. If you are a runner, the chances are you flinched at least once as you read that list. Countless studies have been undertaken to calculate the injury rate for runners: most find that around 50 per cent pick up a running injury each year.

Even if you've been lucky enough to avoid injury, the spectre of them haunts every runner. The merest passing twitch in their legs or feet are enough to tip them into a panic attack, with visions of long lay-offs, culminating in the crocked jogger becoming fat and wheezy, unable to ever retain their former fitness and physique.

Remember...

You will probably get nervous and excited the night before a race, so do not worry if you don't sleep too well. However, the night before the night before the race is widely considered the most important pre-event sleep, so try for a good kip then.

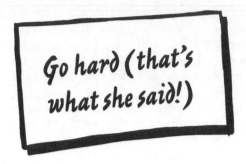

Go hard (that's what she said!)

Funny Spectator Signs at Running Events

Remember...

When you've finished a race/event, the generally held view is that you should rest or at least take it easy out there for one day for each mile you ran.

Runners You Know:
Mr Hands-Free Headset

Of all the times of day you could choose to make phone calls, you opt to get them out of the way during your run. Oh, how lucky the person at the other end of this conversation must feel. What else would anyone want but a phone call from a pumped-up, panting man as he stomps around his local park?

Naturally, of course, this runner particularly likes to make work-based calls during his run. He will bark into his Bluetooth set about 'blue sky thinking', 'keeping the client onside' and other such drivel.

The conversation will be conducted at maximum volume, so everyone else in the park can learn how impressive this person is. I mean, look at him, he can't only run, he also has a job. What a macho man! How lucky the world is to have him in our midst!

Running Myths Reconsidered:
You Cannot Drink Too Much Water

Armchair running coaches will tirelessly advocate for the benefits
of drinking water, arguing that as you sweat your way through
a run it is impossible to drink too much of the stuff. But you
can drink too much. In fact, if you drink too much you will kill
yourself: too much water can cause you to go into hyponatraemia,
which means your salt levels drop too low. Particularly at risk are
smaller runners, and those who mix walking with running over a
long-distance course.

Things We Hate About Running:
Uncooperative Pedestrians

I mean, sure, the fact that I'm in the zone, in the middle of
a 34-kilometre (21-mile) training run is never going to be
as important to random strangers as it is for me. I (slightly
resentfully) accept that. I really do. But honestly, when a family is
walking four abreast along a narrow pavement, would it kill one of
them to step aside slightly and allow me past? I'm convinced that
they would do that if I were walking down the road, so why do
they think it's acceptable, just because I am running, to effectively
push me into the traffic?

Running wanker!

Things People Shout at Runners

Things We Hate About Running: Inane Encouragers

'Not far to go now,' chirps one (in the second mile of a half marathon). 'Mind over matter,' offers another (forgetting that too much 'mind' during a run can actually be the most disruptive thing to your run). Ah, they mean well.

Weird Marathons: Le Marathon du Médoc

This race in Pauillac near Bordeaux offers runners the chance to sample a selection of wines at the 23 tastings along the route. There are also opportunities to eat oyster, cheese and ice cream. Well, it makes a change from water, sports drinks and energy gels. Participants are allowed up to 6 hours 30 minutes to complete the course. What condition they finish in rather depends on how enthusiastically they 'refuel'.

Did you Know?

No fewer than 570 marathons take place in the USA each year. Around 0.5 per cent of the American population has run a marathon.

From Hot to Cold and Back Again

In times gone by, received wisdom was that the best way to relax after a long run was in a deep, hot bath. As they were out pounding the pavement, runners would enjoy imagining the long soak ahead – particularly during winter runs. What could be more agreeable?

But then experts announced that such baths were actually a fast track to injury, because the hot water would exacerbate muscle inflammation. So runners were instead advised to take colder baths, or even to bathe in a tub of ice cubes. On the positive side, this would immediately address any swelling. However, having knocked out mile after mile, the last thing most runners wanted to do was step into a freezing tub.

So the good news is that a study released by Extremes Research Group at Bangor University in Wales has put warmth back in fashion. They found that a hot bath can stimulate the immune system – a particularly important factor during heavy training, which prompts a short-term slump in immunity.

The researchers also concluded that hot baths after a series of runs helped runners to acclimatise to running on hotter days – taking 4.9 per cent off their 5k time in the study. Other benefits of a steamy soak include a reduction in blood pressure and arterial stiffness.

So, when you get back from a long run, simply put in the plug, twist the hot tap and await your orgy of bubbles and heat. You truly deserve it – enjoy!

Things We Hate About Running:
Anyone Who is Better at Running Than Me

How absolutely *dare* they? Get out!

My Running Story:
Author Jenny Baker

I started running because I knew I needed to do some exercise. I kept it up because I found that it gave me so many benefits – better mental health, the opportunity to push myself and achieve new things, a community to belong to in my running club, and lots of good friends. But over the last couple of years I have discovered another dimension to running: a source of life and healing while undergoing treatment for breast cancer.

A cancer diagnosis is terrifying, particularly at first when you don't know any details and it's very easy to imagine the worst. I felt like I'd been shifted into a parallel world where everyone else was carrying on as normal, but I was watching from a distance, unsure about what I could depend on any more. I had thought I was fit and healthy; I was wrong. I was losing my routine, the plans I had made for the year and I felt like my very identity was disappearing. Somehow I knew that I needed to keep on running, and in those early days following my diagnosis my runs were a welcome space where I could start to process what was happening to me. I would set out, my mind an anxious tangle of thoughts and I would arrive back at home feeling calmer and thinking, 'I can do this'.

Gradually a treatment plan emerged. I would need to have chemotherapy first to shrink the tumour. When I went to see my oncologist I had one main question – can I keep running? He said that no one had ever asked him that before but he didn't see why not. It turned out that he was a marathon runner too. In between telling me all the worst side-effects of chemo, he sang the praises of German marathons and told me I should do Berlin next. He also gave me an 18-week plan for chemotherapy – six treatments, three weeks apart with difficult weeks when the drugs would kick in and hopefully an easier week before the next treatment.

I ran to my first chemotherapy appointment, 11 kilometres (7 miles) along the river from Kew Bridge to Hammersmith in

London because I was feeling fit and healthy. Having chemo was like taking a prolonged dive underwater; I felt weak and ill, cut off from normality. Ten days later when I started to feel a bit more like myself again, I did a shaky couple of miles around the common to see whether I could still run. It was hesitant and slow, but it felt fantastic. Over the next week I gradually built up the distance I could run, and ran to my second chemo session with my friend Lucy. I set off weighed down with sorrow and anxiety; I arrived at the hospital having run through sunshine with great conversation, feeling liberated and ready for what was ahead. I resolved to run to all my chemo sessions if I could. Even if I got the Underground most of the way and only jogged the last few hundred metres, I wanted to keep running to my appointments and arrive at the hospital in my trainers and on my terms.

What I discovered was that as well as making you fitter, running helps to build your resilience. Those mornings that you force yourself out of the door for a run even though you don't feel like it; that moment in a race where you stick to your pace when everything in you wants to slow down; that final hill rep that you make yourself do even though you arrive at the top gasping for breath – they all serve to strengthen your character and help you overcome difficulty. They make you less inclined to give up when the going gets tough, and more likely to find ways to cope with the situation in front of you. I found that having a goal to aim for, having friends to run with and having a regular habit of running all gave me a sense of purpose through my treatment and a determination to hold on to what I loved doing.

When you find out you have cancer, you don't get given a manual on how to cope with it, and everyone needs to find their own way through it. Cancer and its treatment are so varied and people respond very differently to what is done to them. What I did won't suit everyone, but I want people to realise that there is no need to stop running just because you have been diagnosed with cancer; if you want to run and you have the energy then you should. All cancer patients have to cope with fatigue, but running has been shown to reduce this rather than cause it. And regular runners who get the same news as I did will be well equipped to cope with what lies ahead of them, because of the habits and character they have developed through their running.

I did run to all my chemotherapy sessions. My sisters, my sons and my friends ran with me to the final one in September and my memory of that day is of the laughter and conversation on the run, not the treatment that came afterwards. Later that year I had a mastectomy and reconstruction, and then radiotherapy and hormone therapy. Through all of that, running kept me going and helped me rewrite the story of what was happening to me.

Jenny Baker is a marathon runner and author who works in the charity sector. Her book about running and cancer, Run for Your Life, *is published by Pitch Publishing.*

Running Philosophy

❝ A lot of people run a race to see who is fastest. I run to see who has the most guts. **❞**
Steve Prefontaine, Olympic runner

Did you Know?

A leg-busting 5164 – the total steps along the Great Wall of China marathon route.

Runners You Know: The walking runner

When does walking become jogging? When does jogging become running? Finally, when does running become sprinting?

The first of these questions springs to mind every time I see what I call a walking runner. Their pace is so slow that it is hard to be sure they are actually running at all. Were it not for the fact they are decked out in running gear, you'd just regard them as someone talking a stroll, albeit with a peculiar gait and mildly urgent approach.

Now I'm all for runners taking everything at their pace. One of the things that plagues the pastime most is pressure on anyone to run faster or harder. And I am fully aware that power walking – brisk walking as a form of aerobic exercise – is a popular thing.

But this is something else. This is a runner who has managed to invent a new type of movement – neither jogging nor walking. This is no small achievement.

So let's hear it for the walking runner. Very much a part of the running community, they are shining examples of what is surely one of the key positive principles in running: taking every step at your pace and to hell with everyone else.

Things We Hate About Running: Sweat Running into the Eyes

I mean, one could wear a Mark Knopfler-esque sweatband to avoid this problem, but that's more suitable for the installation of microwave ovens than running ultramarathons.

Funny Spectator Signs at Running Events

To Greet or Not to Greet?

It is a dilemma that haunts all runners when they see another runner appear on the horizon, moving towards them: do I say hi, or do I not say hi?

Many runners feel it is always pleasant to acknowledge the other person and, without wanting to sound too much like a 94-year-old suburban grandmother, it costs nothing to be polite. Perhaps you could give each other a little boost, simply by saying hi? Just a simple thumbs-up of solidarity can go a long way.

And yet there is no set etiquette for all of this, and some runners prefer not to get involved with greetings, either because they are too shy or too focused on what they are doing. Or they might simply be too grumpy in the moment, reasoning that the 'running brotherhood' concept can quite simply go and screw itself. Once you start saying hi to people, they believe, it's only one step away from them moving in with you, or asking you to mow their lawns for them.

These are difficult issues for which there are no easy answers, as you will often discover when you are out on a run. Between when you first spot the other runner and the moment they pass you, the internal dialogue can go something like this:

'Oh no, will they want me to say hi or not? I mean, I like to say hi, it's lovely to have that moment of connection and solidarity with another runner. But on the other hand what if I say hi and they just blank me. The devastation of being aired! I don't know what to do for the best. No, actually, I think I will say hi. What's the worst that could happen? So what if they ignore me, it doesn't invalidate my existence. Or does it? If I say hi and they don't, they'll probably run off laughing, thinking I'm a right proper loser. And yet if I do say hi, it might seem over-familiar. What if they think I'm trying to become friends with them or even hit on them? This is horrible. Why can't they sod off in a different direction? Then I wouldn't have to even think about all this. Oh no, here they come...'

Make your choice and stick with it. These are big decisions. But don't feel too much pressure. It's only your entire credibility as a runner and human being that is resting on getting it right.

Running Myths Reconsidered: You'll Lose Your Fitness Within Days of Stopping Running

If they are forced to take time off from their favourite hobby, many runners immediately worry they are shedding fitness and form as quickly as an Olympic sprinter polishes off a 100m. However, on his website Runners Connect, expert coach Jeff Gaudette argues that a break from running of less than two weeks isn't likely to affect your fitness level dramatically. Indeed, as numerous experts will tell you, not taking rest days will negatively affect your performance.

Remember...

When you were a beginner runner, you probably had all sorts of rational and irrational fears. Was everyone laughing at you? Would you finish last? What if you fell over? Be nice to the new faces.

I trained for a month to hold this sign!

Funny Spectator Signs at Running Events

Runners You Know: Medal Maniacs

There is a time period within which it is perfectly acceptable, borderline compulsory, some would say, to wear the medal you get at the end of a running event.

Straight after the finish, as you hobble home or back to your hotel, you should certainly wear the medal. For the rest of the day, you could wear your medal. The next day, it might be milking things a touch to continue wearing the medal, but provided the run was a half marathon or longer, then you could keep the shining prize around your neck.

But beyond that? No, it is time to take it off and hang it somewhere. Anything beyond, say, 36 hours after you crossed the finishing line, it is a bad look to be still wearing your admittedly probably hard-won gewgaw.

It might be considered acceptable for elderly war veterans to continue to wear their medals decades on from battle, but they fought in a war, you just ran around a big park a few times.

So, please, don't be the medal maniac. Show some restraint and decorum. Wear it for a bit, post a photo of it on social networks if you must, and then move on. Start planning your next race. Onwards, people, onwards!

Things We Hate About Running: Hunger

Exercise always works up a healthy appetite, particularly outdoor sports. But when you're really putting in the miles each week, the perpetual hunger can become a pain in the neck. Or in the tummy, to be more precise.

Running Philosophy

❝ I've had psychotherapy, I've had group counselling, I've been on and off medication for years, but nothing helped like running. **❞**

Cat Woods, ambassador for England Athletics' #runandtalk scheme

Why Girl Runners are Better

Danish researchers at RunRepeat who studied more than 1.8 million marathon results have found that women slow down less often in marathons than male runners. Although it was initially thought that this was because women's bodies are better at preserving glycogen, subsequent studies have reached a different conclusion. Noting that the same trend was observable in 5ks, in which glycogen preservation is not an issue, experts concluded that women simply make better decisions than men, and are less likely to suffer from overconfidence.

Analysis of official event results also shows that women are three times more likely than men to complete an ultra-running distance.

There are several reasons for this, both biological and psychological. In terms of the former, running coach and movement specialist Shane Benzie says that female runners generally have a larger surface-area-to-mass ratio, which enables heat to dissipate more easily. This means they are better at coping with heat. Moreover, their smaller overall surface area results in lower fluid losses, which in turn means they are less likely to be dehydrated.

In addition, according to *The Complete Book of Running for Women* by Claire Kowalchik (Pocket Books, 1999), women use about 75 per cent more fat than men while running. This affords them a more consistent energy release. It also means that when women take up running they generally experience positive changes in their physique more quickly than men – their legs and back tone up faster, and they lose inches off their waist at a greater pace than males, for instance.

From a mental perspective, when the technology giant Hewlett-Packard researched why more women weren't in top management positions, what they discovered was of interest to runners, too. Female workers applied for a promotion only when they believed they met 100 per cent of the qualifications required, while men were happy to give it a go when they satisfied just 60 per cent of the requirements. This suggests that away from the corporate environment it is possible that female runners won't sign up for a long run unless they feel they are fully prepared and qualified, whereas the more bravado-heavy male is likely to sign up off the back of arrogance as much as suitability.

Whatever the cause for their superiority, the fact is that more and more women are taking part in running events – and they are often the majority. Female runners accounted for 10.7 million finishers in events in the USA in 2014, while just 8 million men finished the same races. This means women represented 57 per cent of event fields.

This is all, though, a very recent shift, since until relatively recently females were simply not permitted to run long distances. For instance, after some women collapsed during the 1928 Olympics 800m race, it was ruled that 200m would be the maximum distance over which women would be allowed to compete. This condescending rule continued until 1960 when the 800m race was reintroduced.

Things weren't much better away from the Olympics, either, and it wasn't until the Pikes Peak Marathon of 1959 that Arlene Pieper became the first American woman to officially finish the distance. Progress was slow from there, with the first ever all-women's marathon being held in Waldniel, West Germany, in 1973. Eleven years later, the first women's Olympic marathon was contested at the 1984 Los Angeles Olympics, and was won by Joan Benoit of the USA.

Numerous female runners have achieved fame and glory since then, not least Britain's most successful female marathon runner of all time, Paula Radcliffe, who won eight of her first ten marathons and became the world record holder in 2003, running 2:15:25 at the London Marathon.

Running Wisdom

A 2014 study by University College London found that exercising three times a week can lower the risk of depression by 16 per cent.

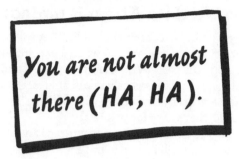

You are not almost there (HA, HA).

Funny Spectator Signs at Running Events

Runners You Know: The Serial Loo Visitor

Portable toilets take quite a battering at large-scale running events. Lines of carbed-up, pumped-up athletes queue to deposit their pre-run anxiety in these cramped chambers, all of which conjures heady conditions inside. Put simply, nobody would tread within a mile of one of these portable loos unless they absolutely *had* to go.

And the serial loo visitor absolutely really, really has to go. He or she will bounce up and down as they queue for the loo, and then no sooner have they finished their business in there, than they have second thoughts and re-join the back of the queue for a sequel visit.

Let's not linger here too long. But before we move on, it's worth noting the gender imbalance that exists. While men can happily take a pee up against trees and walls along the route of running events, women are more or less forced to use the portable loos, which can be scarce. Unfair.

Things We Hate About Running: Dogs

Even the biggest animal lover in the world (that will be me) will struggle to maintain their adoration when a yacking little mutt is chasing you along the park. With their teeth bared and their eyes trained firmly on your exposed calves and ankles, these dogs are trailed by their embarrassed owners, who call out: 'Don't worry, he won't bite!' Well, that's easy for you to say.

The best thing to do in these circumstances is not to try and outpace the dog. That will just encourage it. Instead, you should stop running and use a deep, authoritative voice to take command of the situation. Keep calm. But hey, that's easy for me to say.

Running Philosophy

❝ Don't dream of winning. Train for it. ❞

Sir Mo Farah, CBE, the most decorated athlete in British athletic history

Funny Spectator Signs at Running Events

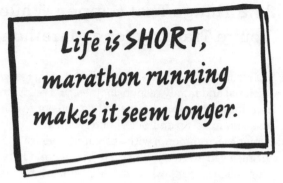

Life is SHORT, marathon running makes it seem longer.

Funny Spectator Signs at Running Events

Runners You Know: Topless Tommy

The moment even a hint of sunshine shows its face in early spring, you whip off your T-shirt and prance along with your pecs out. ('Tommy' can be substituted for a ruder word starting with T, depending on your mood at the time of viewing.)

Remember...

You will never regret taking a bit of toilet paper with you on a long run. But you may well bitterly regret *not* taking any. Enough said.

Go get em!

Things People Shout at Runners

26.2 Things That Happen While You're Training for a Marathon

1. As you struggle to combine a huge weekly mileage with your professional and family responsibilities, you resort to rising at dawn for long pre-work runs. When you get to the office you're so pumped-up and out of kilter with your colleagues that you have arguments with absolutely everyone. Before lunchtime even arrives you're tired, hungry and hated.
2. To your delight, your jawline and neck start tightening and you regularly admire yourself in mirrors. 'Well, check you out,' you say in your head.
3. You pimp out your fundraising page online so often that everyone unfollows you on Twitter and hides you on Facebook. Lots of people say they are going to sponsor you. Some of them even do. Still, it's all for a good cause, right?
4. Whenever you do interval or fartlek training, someone extremely attractive is always walking in front of you. This means you appear at best like someone trying and failing to impress them. Or at worst, it looks like you're repeatedly considering, but then reconsidering, making some sort of scantily clad, sweaty pass at them.

5. You lose any spenders' guilt and splash out on kit, gadgets, pills and gels. You even use some of them. Your email inbox is so full of confirmation emails and dispatch notices you struggle to find any messages sent by actual human beings.

6. Your alcohol tolerance level plummets to that of a teenage experimenter. This means that when you drink with pals you fast-forward to the full-blown, slurred confessional stage somewhere towards the end of your second beer or glass of wine. Just make sure you don't start sending out text messages.

7. During an icy snap you are forced to do your training indoors on a treadmill. Just five minutes into a two-hour run you are so bored that you are tempted to take your chances out in the cold. Don't. Just don't.

8. You catch a cold.

9. You drastically reevaluate your perspective on distance. A half marathon, something you'd previously spend six months preparing for, is now the sort of distance you nonchalantly complete on Tuesday evenings. 10ks become kids' stuff. 5ks? What even are they?

10. On your longer training runs, you suffer from chafing in the most intimate and inconvenient of bodily zones.

11. During one such long run you get all woozy and find yourself struck by an epiphany. When you get home you pile through the front door and share with your partner your new business pitch/screenplay idea/peace plan to resolve the Middle East conflict. They can scarcely understand a word you're saying, and by the time you're in the bath or shower, you realise the sheer insanity of your Big Idea.

12. When you get injured you are secretly thrilled. It gets you a week's guilt-free rest and you can talk to everyone about the minutiae of your strain as if you're some sort of globally recognised Olympic athlete.

13. You compile a playlist of power songs to listen to on your training runs when you need a special psychological boost. It almost certainly includes one out of 'Eye Of The Tiger', 'Simply The Best', 'Sexy and I Know It' and 'You're Beautiful'. My goodness, you cross your fingers nobody finds it.

14. You get carb-loading wrong and for a day or so the only running you get done is to the toilet.
15. Weather forecasts become your new obsession. There is no weather app you don't download and you regularly peruse them, adjusting your training schedule around their predictions.
16. You become depressingly familiar with the defence mechanisms of lazy, overweight non-runners. 'I heard it destroys your knees, 26 miles just seems unnatural, rather you than me,' says one. Another adds: 'Of course, psychologists say that people who run are trying to run away from themselves.' Don't worry, they waddle off in the end.
17. At least once a fortnight, some wag in a white van shouts: 'Run, Forrest, run' at you. Funny, eh?
18. Exhausted all the time, you leave social gatherings as early as politeness permits. You start to prefer quiet nights in, watching TV. You generally fall asleep in front of the box somewhere around 8 p.m. When your partner complains, you tell them: 'I wasn't asleep, it was just a really long blink.'
19. You get another cold.
20. You start your Sunday morning runs so early that you encounter revellers still out from the night before. You were that party animal once. How times change.
21. You get lost during runs, discovering hidden parts of your neighbourhood and feeling like Christopher Columbus in Lycra.
22. As your training programme nears its peak, to your horror you realise that you're actually putting on weight. Thanks to an increase in muscle mass and glycogen storage, plus your tendency to crash out and binge eat after a long run, you begin to gain, rather than lose, pounds.
23. You do, however, lose at least one toenail. First it goes black, then it gets loose, then it comes off. Ewwww.
24. As the physical and mental challenges of it all mount up, you keep yourself motivated by imagining yourself on race day, striding triumphantly towards the finish line, as your proud friends and family cheer you on from the side. (Quick reality check: few, if any of them, will turn up on the day.)

25. With three weeks to go until the marathon itself, you begin the famous taper – drastically reducing your weekly mileage. Even though this is recommended by almost every expert in the world, it feels so wrong to be doing so few miles each week. You repeatedly check online that tapers are definitely the right thing to do. (They are.)

26. Finally, you reach the end of your exhausting, bewildering training programme. Pat yourself on the back – you did it! Now you just have the small matter of the 26.2 miles to complete. Good luck!

26.2. You cannot sleep the night before the event. Don't worry too much – it's the quality of the sleep on the previous night that counts.

Running Philosophy

❝ There will be a lot of suffering and discomfort. Let it hurt. Let it carry me to faster times. **❞**

Alan Webb, who broke the high-school mile record in 1999

Funny Spectator Signs at Running Events

Running Myths Reconsidered:
All Runners are Loners

While it is true that many people veer towards running because it gives them a chance to be alone, it is not true that all who jog are misanthropic loners running away from the rest of our species. Only some of us are. For many, particularly those who join their local running club or become weekly disciples of parkrun, the hobby is more about connection than isolation. With the rise of online running communities and social networks, an evolution is underway and running is becoming an increasingly unifying pursuit.

Did you Know?

One hour of running adds seven hours to your life, according to a study for *Progress in Cardiovascular Diseases*.

Runners You Know:
The Mile-One Maniac

Realistically, the first mile of any medium- to long-distance running event can almost be disregarded. The route is crowded, everyone is a bit overexcited and anxious, and the mile-one maniac is in his or her element.

They will be hustling, jostling and jockeying for position, as if what happens in the first mile has much bearing on what will happen 13 miles later. Some of them will be weaving around other runners like a football winger.

It's all a waste of time and energy. Let them go. They'll be knackered by mile three, and you can have a quiet chuckle as you ease past them.

My Running Story:
Yoga Teacher Indi Singh

I always considered yoga and running as incompatible polar opposites. Like partnering Amma, the embodiment of healing, love and compassion, with Donald Trump, the personification of big ego, self-interest and individual achievement.

For years I had completed races and marathons across the UK and Europe, running against friends, colleagues, strangers, even against the clock. After finishing the London Marathon in a good time, having trained 10 hours a week, it felt like I had reached my pinnacle, of achievement, endurance and, to be honest, interest.

My resignation roughly coincided with a new chapter in my life, yoga, which came as a welcome alternative to the knee-pounding, body-draining, self-obsessive endeavour of racing against others on two legs. I could feel the toll taken on mind, body and soul after years of solo running, and my first gentle steps into the energising, ego-less, love-inducing pursuit of kundalini yoga seemed the right move.

I proudly proclaimed that running was behind me. I hung up my Dry-FIT top, released my bandana and traded them in for linen trousers and a white turban, my new uniform as a kundalini yogi. The focus on 'We' replaced the obsession with 'Me'. In packed classes of seemingly soft, gentle, loving people, my new focus was on physical and mental exercises, with the aim of understanding and deconstructing the self and connecting to a new perspective.

However, after getting married and fathering our firstborn, I realised that the neglect of my physical body was starting to impact the spiritual practice, as my Buddha belly inched further and further outwards. I decided that drastic measures were needed and dusted off my sweat top and trainers to get back on the road to run, this time with a different outlook.

I realised there's not really that much difference between running and yoga. I found the two disciplines could gently jog side by side. Yogic philosophy shows us that the breath and emotions are interrelated. Just as a person's emotional state has an effect on their breath, the inverse is also true. The emotional state can be neutralised by controlling the breath.

As a runner you're also required to build a relationship with the breath, to understand its capacity, range and limit. Once this understanding develops, you can begin to control that relationship to your benefit, to allow for conservation, recovery and even that thrilling final dash across the finish line.

Yogic teachings tell us that unresolved emotional trauma – from loss, abuse or failure – can be stored in the heart, lungs and chest. The yogic solution is to prise open the heart and chest, and strengthen the lungs, using a variety of dynamic or stationary postures and meditations such as bow pose, or camel pose.

Running can operate in a similar way, by working the heart, chest and lungs, and strengthening them in an effective enough way to last the distances you need to cover. As the heart, chest and lungs open over time, trauma and emotional blocks can begin to quite literally be run out of the body.

For many, the practice of yoga is as simple as taking time to sit, alone, in meditation, to quieten the monkey mind. This reduces the energy and prana (life force) taken up by the frenetic nature of the mind so the brain and body can rejuvenate.

In a similar way, when you run, you have the chance to escape the information superhighway of thoughts that processes the mind like a supercomputer. You bring tools of your own; a focus on the breath, on the pace, to zone out with music, or the repetitive bounce of the body. Quietening the mind alone can rejuvenate, even when the body is under physical strain.

Discipline is required for the intense physical and mental exercise of the yogic path, but your heightened awareness and experience confirms that this way of life works. The achieved wisdom that if you don't live the lifestyle, do contradictory things, give in to your vices or laziness, something doesn't feel right.

The same is true as a runner. Your achieved wisdom is no less tangible and dictates that if you live life going against your natural flow, there will be consequences. The heightened awareness of a primed body will bring a very physical regret about last night's beer-and-kebab binge, or the sneaky social smoke after work. Discipline can become a force in a runner's life, and not only to combat the physical challenges. Emotional and psychological walls can come down as one's confidence grows having achieved whatever targets you've set yourself, be they knocking seconds off your mile time or crossing the line at your first marathon.

Each person takes with them their own experiences and wisdom from running or yoga. For those of us who have felt a shift, an emotional release, stress reduction or anything beyond aching legs or exhaustion, the effect can be so tangible it leaves an indelible mark, which keeps us coming back again and again to peel away more and more layers of unnecessary baggage.

Whatever your pursuit of choice, be it yoga, running or both, the question perhaps should not be whether the two can co-exist, rather what mindset one brings to either, or both. Where are your thoughts in any given moment? Where is your focus? A lesson in life for doing anything and everything.

Indi Singh is a former amateur marathon runner turned professional yogi turned full-time father turned runner again. He's run races in France, Germany and the UK, including the London Marathon. Indi is also a qualified yoga teacher with a strict daily spiritual discipline.

Always give **100** per cent – apart from when giving blood.

Funny Spectator Signs at Running Events

Weird Marathons:
North Korea Marathon

Perhaps the planet's most reclusive country has recently begun to allow foreigners to take part in its annual marathon. So if secretive, dictatorial regimes are your thing, then this is the 26-miler for you. The event, which begins and ends in Kim Il-sung Stadium in Pyongyang, is part of annual birthday celebrations for the former North Korean leader, which doesn't feel creepy at all.

Runners You Know: The Vegan Marathon Runner

Q: How do you know if someone's a vegan and run a marathon?
A: I'll tell you.

Running Wisdom

❝ It's hard to run and feel sorry for yourself at the same time. Also, there are those hours of clear-headedness **❞** that follow a long run.

Monte Davis, Runner

Funny Spectator Signs at Running Events

How to Beat Your 5k PB

Set realistic targets

Let's say your current PB is around 22 minutes. Aiming to jump straight to a sub-20 minute finish would be to set yourself up for crashing disappointment. Instead, try to knock 10 seconds off the previous Saturday's finish time each week. That's just two seconds faster per kilometre – a realistic target.

You may find yourself knocking more than that off some weeks, and the satisfaction of bettering your target will fire your enthusiasm.

Try a new venue

It's only when you try a new park or venue that you realise how many ruts you've become stuck in at your regular haunt: that boringly familiar slope in the second kilometre that saps your enthusiasm, the over-friendly parkrunner whose hellish mid-run 'banter' always throws you, the running jokes that have got old.

So find a new event, familiarise yourself with the course on its website, and prepare to soar when you get there.

Do your intervals

Interval training builds both speed and muscular endurance, so work some into your weekly schedule.

You can measure it out by time: run 120 seconds at full pelt, followed by two to three minutes of easy jogging. Or by distance: run 4 x 1km at full pace, with two-minute easy jogs between each kilometre.

Fancy a less structured approach? Try the enjoyably-named 'fartlek', in which you choose your own milestones on the hop: you might decide to run hard to the lamp post ahead, then slow down until the traffic lights, and then burst forwards again until the train bridge.

Check your posture

If you still need convincing on the importance of posture, just leave your kit at home one week and watch a parkrun from the sidelines. You will notice that the runners who finish at the front almost invariably have better posture than those who are further back.

The front pack will have: an upright posture, relaxed shoulders, their trunks as still as possible, and their hips forward. Their arms will move in a linear, rather than outward, direction, and their feet will land under their centre of gravity. Learn from them.

Find a pacer event

Some running events hold pacer weeks, in which clearly marked volunteers pace specific finishing times from 19 minutes upwards. This makes it all a lot simpler: there'll be no need for you to check your stopwatch or calculate how you are doing – just stick by the pacer for the time you want to finish in.

Fast to run fast

Many experts advise not eating at all on the morning of a 5k. Provided you follow a generally healthy diet and ate sensibly the previous evening, your body should have enough glycogen stored to more than see you through 5k without breakfast.

If you prefer to get something down you, make it a light snack, taken around 90 minutes before the run starts. And whether you eat or not, make sure you drink up to 500ml (17fl oz) water ahead of start time.

Don't chat – warm up

As parkrunners assemble each week, they generally break into one of two camps. First, there are the chatterers. They gossip, put the world to rights, indulge in a spot of one-upmanship and eventually plod towards the starting line. The second camp, meanwhile, have been stretching and warming up – finely tuning their bodies and minds for the activity ahead.

If you want a faster time you have to be in the second camp.
Start your warm-up 15 minutes before the run, and finish
five minutes before the starting pistol. Focus. You can do your
chatting afterwards.

It's ace to pace

Some parkrunners swear by the 'start fast and try and hang on'
approach. Others prefer the negative split, in which they run at
a slightly conservative pace for the first half and then attack the
course in the second half. The trouble with the first approach is
that it's unnecessarily masochistic, and the second one requires
discipline and mid-run mathematics.

Simpler than both is the even-pace approach. Work out what
your average pace needs to be for your target time, and stick to
that with the help of your running watch.

Start right

Parkruns do not use chip times, so if you go over the start line five seconds after the pistol sounds, that five seconds will be added to your time. Make sure you position yourself as close to the front as you can get.

It's (nearly) all in the mind

One week at parkrun I changed the way I mentally charted my progress. As I passed the first kilometre marker, rather than telling myself 'You've run the first k', I told myself: 'You're in the second k.' This simple mental trick, which made me feel I was further ahead, gave me such encouragement that I knocked 38 seconds off my previous week's finish time.

Other runners find a reverse countdown works: 5, 4, 3, 2, 1...

Demolish the last half-k

Whether you went for a faster first half, a negative split, an even-paced run, or had no overall tactic, there is no reason not to absolutely ruin the last 400m or so. Take a deep breath and run as hard as you can until you pass the finish line.

Remember...

Jogging on the spot at traffic lights is unnecessary and silly. When you are out running and are forced to wait at traffic lights, or at the side of a busy road, there is the temptation to either jog on the spot or bounce up and down – anything to keep the movement going. But is this necessary? No. And it looks a bit desperate. So just chill for a bit. You'll soon be on the move again.

Pick it up!

Things People Shout at Runners

Remember...

It's not all about you. When you are out pounding the pavements it's easy to run away with the idea that everyone is looking at you. But before you become a self-conscious mess, glance around and notice that actually, the fact you are out running is not making a huge difference to anyone else's day. No one cares about you – so stop worrying and revel in your irrelevance!

Did you Know?

A staggering 26 bones, 33 joints, 112 ligaments and a complex group of nerves, tendons, and blood vessels are all active when you run.

Notable Runners:
Sir Roger Bannister, CH, CBE

After winning gold medals at the Commonwealth Games and European championships, in 1954 Bannister became the first person to break the four-minute mile barrier.

Runners You Know: The Analyser

The natural habitat for the analyser is that car park at a parkrun or similar running event. There they will be dissecting their run as if they're the man of the match, being quizzed on a satellite sports channel.

'As I've passed the 3k marker I've really put my foot down and given it some but then I've paid the price in the final stretch,' they say, as if anyone anywhere cares in the least. 'I could feel my left calf twitching and then my breathing's gone. I've given it 100 per cent but I suppose it just wasn't to be my day. I think ultimately I've set off too strongly. When it comes down to it, I should have kept some fuel in the tank for the big finish. It's all swings and roundabouts, really...'

Thanks for that. It's always good to hear the minutiae of your run. It's all we come along for, really.

There's just so much to think about. Could taking that corner slightly more slowly have ultimately reduced the rebalancing in the stretch ahead of it, thus shaving an all-important 40 seconds off your finishing time? Now, there's something to think and chat about all weekend!

Might it be better to have taken breakfast 30 minutes earlier? Or not to have eaten breakfast at all? Is it better to go for it in the first half of the parkrun, or to wait until the second half and then gallop like a horse on amphetamines?

As well as thinking about these questions, the analyser witters on about them, even as their fellow runners gently slip away to their cars, to their weekends. Meanwhile, the analyser keeps banging on. Pray for their family.

'The conditions probably played a part, though. For me, I've always said spring is the best time and today I could have just done with it being 2°C (3.6°F) hotter. Then my finish time would have been better for sure, for sure. I remember this one time when...'

Well, if nothing else, analysers do perform a service to other runners. Terrified of being stuck with him or her in the car park afterwards, they will run a bit faster each week, in the hope of getting away before the navel-gazing post-run monologue can begin.

Weird Marathons:
Burro Days World Championship
Pack Burro Race

Here is a run in which you must, quite literally, drag your ass around the course. In homage to the region's Goldrush era, all competitors in this Colorado-based off-road marathon must race with a donkey bearing 15kg (33lb) of mining gear. It describes itself as a cruelty-free event, and anyone using prods, whips or other harsh encouragers is immediately disqualified.

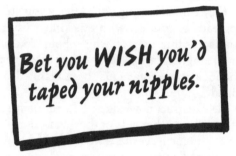

Bet you WISH you'd taped your nipples.

Funny Spectator Signs at Running Events

Remember...

If a dog snaps at your ankles as you are out running, its owner will probably be quietly approving.

Things We Hate About Running:
Friendly/Unfriendly Runners

You know the drill: you're enjoying an effortless, graceful run on a beautiful spring morning, as your local park begins to bloom. You feel athletically in the zone, but so much more than that. You are in tune with nature, your endorphins are flowing, your mind is alive and happy.

And then, in the distance, you see a brother or sister – a fellow runner. He or she must surely be in the same 'place' as you, experiencing every bit of the joy flowing through you. We're all one ball of love after all, are we not?

And here they come, moving your way as you stride along. You look up, ready to connect with this kindred spirit, ready to merge your souls into one, glowing whole. You smile, and say: 'Good morning!' In return, they screw up their face with derision, and look away. You've just been blanked, and your mood is ruined.

Some people like to acknowledge fellow runners, some do not. A lot of us fall on either side of the divide, depending on our mood in the moment. Perhaps we're in a bad mood, or we're using our run to mull over a difficult issue. Or maybe we're just feeling plain shy. It can feel invasive to have to acknowledge chirpy passers-by.

The whole do I/don't I acknowledgement issue adds a social pressure to running that I could do without. [See: To Greet or Not to Greet on page 110.]

Runners You Know:
The Spiritual Runner

Your face is starry eyed and blissful. It's spaced out and serene. There's also something a little preachy about it. The spiritual runner, like their religious equivalent, wants the whole world to know how great life can be if they follow their path.

And the spiritual runner's path winds around the local park. That's where you can find this runner. Their face, rather than the exhausted, contorted, wheezing mess of some joggers, is instead a thing of blissed-out wonder.

When you see a spiritual runner, your reaction will depend on your mood on the day. Feasting your eyes on this joyful jogger, you may feel such admiration, connection and love that emotion will flow through you as you regard such a happy soul. Good on them, you might think, for finding something so simple to make them happy.

Or, if you're in a grumpy mood, you might want to smash them in their glazed, self-satisfied face.

Not that the spiritual runner would mind, of course. Because, man, running has put them in such a focused, centred state, with their chakras all aligned and their place in the universe clarified, they would merely turn the other cheek.

They are so flushed with endorphins that they are as happy as they can be and the only fair thing to do is let them bask in it. So if you see one, leave them to enjoy their rapture.

The Joy of Solitude

'And if you say run, I'll run with you...' So sang the late, great David Bowie. I wish I could say (or even sing) the same, but for me, the best runs are the ones I do alone.

There are now so many ways to *not* be alone when you run. You could join a running club, find a jogging buddy, or take out your smartphone with you so you can be phoned, or sent emails, mid-dash.

But who wants any of that? For many of us, one of the best things about running is the serenity and solitude of it.

There are so many advantages:

1. The freedom to roam – you can determine your own route and pace as you meander along. You are also entirely free of the tyranny of a set weekly start time for your run, or the complexity of arranging a run with a friend.
2. You avoid small-talk hell – seriously, when you're 8 kilometres (5 miles) into a run, who wants some prat panting away into your ear about his tax affairs or the extension he is thinking of getting at his pad?
3. Choose your own soundtrack – instead of being bored to tears, you can listen to music, or power through audio books or podcasts, or just simply run in peace.
4. Learn self-sufficiency for the big day – if you've had plenty of practice running on your own you'll be able to find and maintain a pace that works for you. In contrast, if you run mob-handed you may end up relying on others for a boost when you get tired or sore. The power of your self-sufficiency could prove a great asset on race day because the same person will be encouraging you then as is during your training – you.
5. Let's bliss out – running alone can become a positively meditative experience, particularly over longer distances.
6. Inner dialogue can be very therapeutic – many a problem can be solved by taking a long solitary run while thinking it over.
7. No competitiveness – running clubs and running partners seem to bring out many runners' unseemly, competitive side.

All those middle-aged sprints to the finish aren't as good a look as those participating in them would have you think. Leave that to them, and instead enjoying competing against no one but yourself.

8. You don't have to shower beforehand – if you're running in a group you may feel obliged to wash first and wear pristine kit, which feels excessive when you know you're going to shower afterwards too. You can be as sweaty as you like when you're running alone.

9. Noticing your form – when you're running with a friend or a pack it is hard to pay full attention to your pace, breathing and overall form. Go out on your own and you can really focus on how you are doing and what is going on for you.

10. Wind – sorry to lower the tone but any runner who eats lots of healthy food is going to need to pass gas on a reasonably frequent basis. When you are running alone you can let rip with impunity, grunting at will without embarrassment or concern. A plus!

11. Being present – when you're alone you can truly live in the moment and observe nature more deeply.

Did you Know?

Twenty-two minutes – that's how long you will need to run for at a speed of 8km/h (5mph) in order to burn off the calories in an average chocolate bar, according to the Royal Society for Public Health.

Running Philosophy

“ It's called the 'runners' high' – we don't hear the term 'cyclists' high' or 'rowers' high'. This could be because running is an extension of movement humans learn naturally as babies. It's also rhythmic, so possibly there's a meditative quality to it. **”**

Andy Lane, professor of sports psychology at the University of Wolverhampton

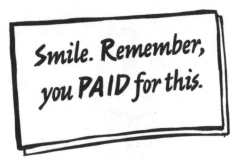

Smile. Remember, you PAID for this.

Funny Spectator Signs at Running Events

My Running Story:
Parkrun Founder Paul Sinton-Hewitt CBE

As long as I can remember I have been a runner. Not an athlete, just a runner. The kind of person who heads out on a run with little thought about the performance but rather concentrating on the experience instead.

However, the more you do something, the better you get at it and the probability is that you then start focusing on the performance.

My first recollection of realising that running was good for me occurred in my early 20s. I competed on the track and at cross-country at school and I did OK. Not good enough to achieve school colours for my achievements but good enough to be a part of the team. On reflection, I wasn't aware of the emotional benefits I was receiving at the time. That would come later on.

Throughout my late teens and early 20s, I occasionally ran. Sometimes it was part of a workout, mostly when doing my basic training in the air force, but sometimes it was simply for myself. Something told me that the occasional run was good for me; for my physical health and also for my mental state. And so I would simply put on a pair of plimsolls (we called these tackies in South Africa in the late '70s) and head out. It wasn't until I was working as a software programmer for a large bank and stuck with a work problem that I felt I couldn't solve that I truly discovered the power of running.

My approach to most things has always been to apply total dedication and commitment, and work life was no different. When offered a problem to solve I would throw myself into the analysis, design and problem solving with complete focus. Having unsuccessfully wrangled with this particular issue for a couple of weeks and reached the point of giving up, I headed out for my midday run. The solution to the issue came to me towards the end of my session. Grateful for the revelation I headed straight back to work and quickly coded the solution, and returned home later in the day victorious.

Since then, there have been many occasions when going for a run has led to a better state of mind. My work in the '90s and early noughties involved a great deal of travel, intense projects with tight deadlines and important stakeholder management. I used to pride myself on my ability to handle the high levels of stress. Older and wiser now, I can reflect and it's quite evident that without the occasional run I might not have coped so well.

In my running life, I have competed against others with gusto, determined to be the best I could be over the chosen distance. I have trained hard and I have raced hard. That part of my life has passed and is confined to history now. Today, I relish the opportunity to head out into a beautiful park, along the river or some undiscovered path just for the experience. And the truth is that while I am not very stressed any more I still find myself benefitting enormously from the whole experience. Ultimately, running makes me healthier and happier.

Paul Sinton-Hewitt, CBE, is the founder of parkrun.

Remember...

Even though some say that runners improve for about seven years, that is no excuse to not keep at it, or to avoid trying new things. Especially because, according to *Runners World*, low-mileage runners can stretch the seven years to well over a decade before plateauing sets in.

Runners You Know:
The Kid With Really Baggy Shorts

He's a kid. He wears really baggy shorts. That's it, really.

Runners You Know: The Child Runner

At just nine years of age, she or he still manages to finish near the front of the pack. How? Your legs are tiny!

Things We Hate About Running:
Bugs in the mouth

There you are, out running in the forest on a hot, sunny day. You've remembered to wear your running glasses, mostly because you don't want bugs flying into your eyes. So that's the bug problem solved, right? Well, the trouble is that to complete a run, you kind of have to breathe, and every time you do, a bug flies into your mouth. An early luncheon.

(Non) Runners You Know:
The Runner's Widow

You can say what you like about the tribulations of the runner's widow, and in a moment I really shall, but you also have to look at the upside. As Big Ben ushers in each New Year, the widow can map out their entire year to the letter. Every sodding day is accounted for.

Take Saturdays, for instance. All 52 Saturday mornings can be marked out on the calendar, as the widow's wife or husband attends parkrun. Heck, Saturday afternoons are pretty much determined for the year, too. The widow will spend them listening to their partner prattle on and on (and on and on) about that morning's parkrun, their finish time and how they think they will better it next week.

Think you'll get to see the runner of the family on Sunday? After all, they were out running on Saturday – surely they'll need a rest? Duh! Parkruns are mere 5km affairs, more of a gentle warm-up than anything depleting. No, Sundays are another running day – often the main one of the week. So don't get any ideas about enjoying a Sunday roast and a glass of wine. Instead, it will be all about rice cakes and bananas.

Any holidays will either have to be slotted in around parkruns, or taken in areas that also have a parkrun, and plenty of suitable locations for training, so the runner can spend much of the break out there alone, running along cliff tops, beach promenades or forests, in a movie of their own mind. If the widow and their children are lucky, they may spot the runner of the family, as he or she speeds along on another 18-miler.

Yet the widow experience is not confined to weekends and holidays – it's a daily experience. Each day begins early, with the runner leaping out of bed before dawn to get some food down their gullet ahead of an early run. Breakfast in bed, romantic dawns, or even a basic lie-in are all out of the question.

On and on the runner trots, pounding pavements every day of the week, before returning home and performing balletic stretches, unaware of family life continuing all around them. Their habit is all-consuming and allows little time for paying attention to the partner and kids.

There are three in the marriage – and for the running widow, life is slightly more bearable when the third party is available. And while it's true that the widow feels slighted that only running seems able to transform their partner's mood from gloomy to chipper, at least something can do the trick. And hey, it's cheaper than therapy, I hear...

Things People Shout at Runners

Running Philosophy

❝ It feels like it's a weapon. It's something that you have. It means you can dictate in a race, it's important. You're in control. **❞**

Sir Mo Farah, CBE

Did you Know?

The average pace for runners in Glasgow in 2015 was 5:17 minutes per kilometre (8:28 minutes per mile), making it the fastest city in the UK that year, according to Strava.

Running Wisdom

A study by the *International Journal of Sports Physiology and Performance* found that positive, motivational self-talk led to a faster 10k time trial than when self-talk was neutral. Moreover, while the runners worked harder, their perception of their level of exertion was unchanged.

Funny Spectator Signs at Running Events

Runners You Know:
The Interval Trainer

To non-runners, or any aliens that have beamed down from outer space, this athlete probably seems like the most indecisive person on the planet. First they run fast for a bit, then they run slowly for a bit, then fast again, but then slow once more. Why can't they just make up their mind? (Were the runner to explain: 'No, it's just that I'm doing a fartlek,' this would be unlikely to clarify things for the aforementioned non-runner/alien.)

Did you Know?

A total of 80 per cent of men and 60 per cent of women actually felt more attractive due to regular running, according to a study of 408 participants by the University of Arkansas.

Runners You Know: The Loving Couple

The couple that runs together stays together, goes the age-old saying. Okay, it isn't actually a saying. I just made it up. But according to a Brooks Running survey of 1000 adults who run at least once a week, running as a couple can enhance your sex life.

The study found that 66 per cent of runners believe they have more sex when they run with their partner. Presumably not during the run, though. Slightly weirdly, men (71 per cent) were more likely than women (just 62 per cent) to notice the connection. Do they know something their wives don't?

More sober research flagged up a connection between couples who exercise together and longevity. A 2000 study found that after jointly participating in a physical challenge or activity, couples felt more satisfied with their relationships and more in love with their partner.

And as far back as 1983, researchers Bond and Titus found that the presence of your partner on a run will boost your speed. You

may not even be aware of their influence, they concluded, such is the seamless way this proximity works. In the previous decade, Dutton and Aron found that because exercise brings on some of the symptoms of romantic arousal – sweaty hands, a faster pulse, shortness of breath – you can mistake this for actual sexual arousal. So the finishing line for a romantic run could well be found between the sheets.

More generally, and less erotically, the experience of running with a partner means that you are mirroring one another's physical posture and movements, bringing you closer. But you don't need to tell the running couple this. They have almost become as one.

As a result, you either love running couples or you hate them. Or, to put it more prosaically, you either wonder at the very strength and purity of their bond and harmony, or you think them a pair of smug sods who rub your face in their perfection with their very existence.

One day, a running-themed rom-com could be made about such a couple. *Four Parkruns and a Marathon*, perhaps. Or *Bridget Jones' Running Journal*. Actually, that could work. Renée Zellweger is probably doing some anticipatory stretches as you read this...

Weird Marathons:
Big Five Marathon

If running with horses or donkeys isn't a bestial-enough experience for you then why not give this one a go? Set in one of the most stunning game reserves in the world in the savannahs of South Africa, you will run among the 'Big Five' of African game: elephants, rhinos, buffalos, lions and leopards. Nothing separates you from these creatures, a fact that may encourage you to trot along a tad faster than normal.

What is the Best Day of the Week to Run?

Monday
A good run is a fine way to shake off any Monday blues.

Tuesday
Statistically, this is the wettest day of the week. But then you may like a wet run.

Wednesday
Researchers found that Wednesday is the most miserable day of the week. So run it off, dude.

Thursday
According to experts, cortisol levels are at their peak.

Fridays
Roads are most dangerous on Friday. So it's better to be running around your park than crawling around a ringroad.

Saturday
Saturday is parkrun day – therefore it's definitely a good day to run.

Sunday
You get to skip lunch with the relatives.

Remember...

It is terribly useful to take in a combination of carbohydrates and protein within 30–60 minutes after any race, speed workout or long run.

Things We Hate About Running:
Bug Paranoia

Like all runners, I hate missing out on my regular jogs. As a result, I'm eternally vigilant for anything that could put me out of action. But while I can keep an eye out for big obstacles and dangers, there's not much I can do if someone lets out an untethered sneeze on a packed train.

Now to be fair, few people actively want to catch a cold or come down with flu. However, for runners, such bugs are a particularly savage blow: annoying for all the normal reasons and then annoying all over again because they take away our favourite activity from us. (Unless, that is, we are one of those runners who will take to the roads even when we're burning up with flu. [See 'The Addict' on page 166.])

26.2 Things That Happen When You Run a Marathon

1. As you mill around at the start, you overhear marathon veterans passing the time with ostentatious one-upmanship. 'I see the weather's not as good as Melbourne 2001,' says one, wearing a T-shirt from a distant marathon. 'Indeed, but at least it's better than Stockholm '97,' agrees another. They both look round to see how many first-timers were listening.
2. You cave in to peer pressure from your pals and go for a pee before you set off, even though you don't really feel like one. As you queue for the Portaloo, you feel a little like your childhood self, going to the loo before a long car journey, just because Mum told you to.
3. After the starting gun sounds, one runner gets completely overexcited and rushes through the starting line as if he's taking on Usain Bolt in a 100m sprint. Just a few hundred metres later he is having a choke on the side of the road. He's got a long day ahead of him.
4. During the crowded first mile any illusions that a male runner has that running a marathon will turn him into an Adonis are shattered as he looks out over a bubbling ocean of male-pattern baldness, skinny arms and protruding Adam's apples.
5. In mile two you notice a growing queue for the loos and feel secretly smug that you went early.
6. You get overtaken by men, it's nearly always men, wearing wacky costumes: a rabbit, a big tomato and at least two Batmen. What personalities, eh?
7. A spectator shouts: 'Keep going – you're nearly there!' You're in mile three, FFS. You're so livid at this vacuous 'support' that you feel like stopping and shouting at them.
8. A skinny, officious man elbows his way past you, muttering something about 'race etiquette'. Cheer up, love.
9. Drinks stations become potential death traps (not literally). Discarded plastic cups, foil gel wrappers and banana skins are strewn all over the pavement as distracted runners speed through the area. The fact that everyone doesn't end up in a

huge pile of mangled bodies with broken skinny limbs suggests that God loves runners.

10. You keep getting overtaken by old men in jogging vests that reveal lots of grey arm hair. You die a bit each time. [See: 'The Inexplicably Good Old Runner' on page 13.]

11. Each time you see a race volunteer you want to thank them from the bottom of your beating heart. But you worry it may be patronising. Was that a little tear emerging from your eye? No, just some optic sweat, surely. Ahem...

12. You worry that worrying about patronising volunteers is using up vital energy.

13. Spectators wave banners and placards as you run past, with slogans such as 'Go Daddy!', 'You're all winners' and 'The Lord is my shepherd, I shall not be in want.'

14. If you're a chap and you spot a speedy runner of the opposite sex whose fetching derrière is squeezed into a rather tight pair of shorts, you are likely to join the large gaggle of men who are running breathlessly just behind her. Later that day, your wife will ask how you managed to complete the course so quickly. 'What can I say,' you'll shrug.

15. A runner collapses and is carried into an ambulance. You think about him, lying in that ambulance, and feel so sad for him.

16. Eventually, the noise and the crowds cease to spur you on and start to actually freak you out a bit. You weren't prepared for this: for months and months you've trained in solitude and relative peace – now you're suddenly surrounded by thousands of people.

17. You pass the 20-mile mark. You think about ambulance guy, lying in that ambulance, and feel so jealous of him.

18. The route passes a branch of your favourite restaurant chain. You look through the window and see people sitting down on a seat, putting food into their mouths. You suddenly feel hungrier than you ever have before.

19. Your nipples start to bleed. You glance down and realise you look like you're lactating blackcurrant juice.

20. Actually, saying that, you could demolish a blackcurrant juice right now. You imagine that lovely cold, sweet drink, slipping down your throat...

21. People start to poo themselves. Like actually poo themselves. Some content themselves with a small spray inside their shorts, others plump for a colourful leak down the back of their legs. The more committed self-defecators go for a full 'Paula Radcliffe'.
22. A mixture of exhaustion, pain, fear and elation mean you start to feel really emotional. You're in pain but you know the end is coming and that somehow you will stick it out. You start to sob uncontrollably. Well, at least you're not pooing yourself, I suppose.
23. You 'hit the wall', meaning your glycogen stores are gone and you feel apocalyptically exhausted. Somehow, it doesn't feel like the end is coming. The end now feels further away than it did in mile one. Damn.
24. Somehow, you eventually pass the finishing line. For months you've imagined that this moment will bring feelings of enormous elation, accomplishment and pride. It's all of that and much, much more. What a moment in your life.
25. You stumble around with your fellow finishers, all wrapped in silver foil capes. You look like recently released avian hostages from a factory farm. You try and find your well-wishers among the crowd. You feel a little panicky and claustrophobic.
26. As you hobble home or back to your hotel in a haze, clutching various refuelling food and drink, three words form clearly in your head: 'never, ever again'. That's it. Your marathon days are over. It's 5ks and no more from now on. There is no doubt in your mind.
26.2 A bath and a rest later, you go online to find the next marathon you can enter.

Remember...

Lining up in the wrong finishing-time pen is kind of cheating. Some running events arrange for participants to line up at the start according to their anticipated finishing time, the theory being that it is better to start alongside people who will be running at your pace. But some runners will cheekily line up in a faster section, so they can get through the first mile with fewer people around them. This is naughty and annoying. Stop it.

Running Myths Reconsidered: Running in Cold Weather is Inherently Bad For You

This myth has been doing the rounds for so long it is approaching old wives' tales proportions. So let's get this straight: you're more likely to catch a cold if you stay inside in the warm, because that's where cold and flu germs fly around like thriving demons. So layer up your running clothes and get out there. [See also: 'Why Winter Running Rocks' on page 99.]

Run, Fatboy, Run!

Things People Shout at Runners

Things We Hate About Running:
Puddle Splashers

Okay, I'm sure that it was just an accident when that car suddenly swerved towards the pavement and sped through that puddle, sending a huge tidal wave my way, just as I'm jogging past it. In fact, I'm here to say that every time it happens, it is entirely unintentional. Even when the car is full of sniggering, gesticulating young men. Yes, they definitely didn't mean to splash me. I mean, why would they? They probably didn't even notice it happened.

Running Philosophy

❝ As every runner knows, running is about more than just putting one foot in front of the other; it is about our lifestyle and who we are. **❞**

Joan Benoit Samuelson, winner of the first ever women's Olympic marathon in 1984

Did you Know?

One billion pairs of running shoes are sold each year.

Runners You Know: The Gobber

This is a less than pleasant topic. So if you are queasy or easily offended, feel free to sprint to the next entry.

The gobber spends their run doing what really matters – emptying out their throat and sinuses. Some go for a reasonably straightforward single-nostril evacuation. By closing one side and pushing hard through the other, they can fire out a reasonable amount of gunk. Hopefully they will have leaned forwards a bit, so the aforementioned mess doesn't land all over their running T-shirt and legs. Because that would suck.

More committed snotters will opt for a two-fingered approach. Here, they squeeze the top of the nose and fire out of both nostrils at once. This one is more likely to result in the stringy mess landing on them, particularly if they are moving at some speed.

The entry level of all this stuff, meanwhile, is the simple spit. However, whichever approach the gobber takes, such expectoration makes for a fairly unpleasant sight – and sometimes sound – for their fellow harriers.

Also for spectators. If you stand at the end of a parkrun, you will notice that some of the faster finishers often cross the finishing line with drool all over their face and neck. Which certainly takes the edge off the glamour of being such a speedy runner. They don't put images of streaming noses on the cover of running mags – and for good reason.

However, gobbers may well point out the physiological fact that to swallow, you have to stop breathing. During short, fast running events, participants may prefer to therefore deal with excess saliva in the most efficient, albeit unsightly, way. Some of those who spit feel that anyone who does not understand is merely not running hard enough – or they would immediately empathise.

And from the gobber's point of view, a hidden plus side of their practice is that they have no need for maps or apps, as they can find their way back home via the slithering trail they have left behind on their training run.

Let the gob guide you home. Just be careful not to slip on it, guys and gals.

My Running Story:
Comedian Paul Tonkinson

I've been running off and on for 34 years. When I was a kid, life was constant movement. I'd wake up, run down to the shop, do my paper round, cycle to school, play football at lunch time, cycle back, come home, go for a run. I was the kid at the front of the cross-country pack, head down, drawing away from the field.

Running was a singular pursuit that I was good at. It gave me a feeling of joy, power and a fleeting freedom. I joined a club, ran for my county and geared my life around it. I kept a diary, ran every day, sometimes twice and competed on the track, over the country and on the roads. Looking back, it was an escape for me, I was running away from an atmosphere at home that could often be described as angry chaos. My running life was incredibly intense but, to be honest, only sporadically truly enjoyable as it was underpinned by an angsty need to run. There was really no option. I had to do it.

Throughout my 20s and 30s I ran occasionally, for intense periods, usually at times of extreme stress. Running was a corrective for other excesses. It cleaned me up after a drinking session, it gave me a lift when down. It's an oft-repeated truism that you never feel worse after a run. You always feel better. To me, an hour's run, especially in nature, rinses the mind of any confusions or depressive thoughts. It realigns me wonderfully with the universe, connects me to others. It reminds me that I am, at root, an animal. I was created to move, to feel the earth beneath my feet, to sweat and work.

A few years ago I began to run more seriously again. I'd done a few marathons and started to feel the urge to improve, to see if I could approach the heights of my youth. It's different now, I'm coming from a happier place. I'm no longer running from anything. Running is instead a gift that I give to myself. It's soul food and I'm incredibly grateful for it. I love the simplicity of it, its tangible nature. Part of the attraction to me is that running offers an area of life over which I can exert some level of control. Family life is chaotic. Work life is glorious but unpredictable. When I run, if I train hard, I will gain my reward. It's very simple.

When I have an event in the diary that I'm training for it clears my mind. Everything incongruous falls away. I'm not stopping drinking alcohol because it affects my running; I'm running, I'm very fit, so my body doesn't want to drink. It's a clear structure that holds me. I feel leaner, my senses clearer, my mind more creative, so it has a wonderful spill-over into creative endeavours.

Part of it for me as well is a good old-fashioned return to childhood. I've re-joined a club. I love going to track sessions on a Tuesday to be with like-minded souls, warming up, pushing ourselves, under the floodlights. Don't get me wrong though, it's pretty intense. I'll be there nearing the end of a track session, approaching my 10th 800m rep, swaying in a line of other runners on a freezing cold night watching my breathe flume out in front of me, gasping for air in the last 10 seconds of recovery before launching into the final three minutes. It's pretty unhinged. But the time elapses, the watch beeps and you launch off round the track. It's a glorious abandonment to physical pain.

Sometimes I laugh at the lunacy of it. What are we doing here? The fact is, it's very pleasurable. To line up at a race with club mates is to propel yourself into a furious joy and to finish the course, after giving everything is to succumb to a blessed relief and a feeling of utter serenity. To be honest it's a feeling I get after a very good gig. Utterly cleansed, connected, alive and suffused with a deep peace. It's as if everything that separates me from others has fallen away. It's hard to describe but let's face it, it's a feeling I'm totally addicted to!

Paul Tonkinson is a 47-year-old stand-up comedian who recently ran a marathon in 2.59.21; a Runner's World *columnist; and appears on* Running Commentary – *the podcast for runners, by runners, recorded while running.*

Weird Marathons:
Tromsø Midnight Sun Marathon

This event takes place in the evening, and the majority of runners complete the course around midnight. However, because the sun doesn't set in this region of Arctic Norway between May and July, the evening run is done in broad daylight. Including the bridge of Tromsø and stunning views of Arctic mountains, it is a breathtaking course in more ways than one.

Remember...

Received wisdom has it that a headwind always slows you down more than a tailwind speeds you up. It's just one of those ways that life can suck.

Things We Hate About Running:
Antisocial Aspects

When you're training for a long-distance run, your preparations can dominate your life for many months in advance. With many runners preferring to do their longest run of the week on either a Saturday or Sunday, this can effectively knock you out of the partying loop for large parts of the year.

So, when your workmates are headed to the pub or bar for a Friday night sundown drink, you find yourself making excuses. The same goes for any big bashes over the weekend. You either take it easy, sipping a few gentle drinks and heading home early, or dodge the gig altogether. Neither move makes you all that popular with the party-animal brigade, but sometimes you cannot please both your friends and your training log.

Did you Know?

Researchers at Durham University found that runners who wear red are more likely to win during competitions.

Runners You Know:
The Treadmill Terrier

This runner is all about the treadmill life. They've never run outdoors, apart from that one time they were late for a train. Instead, they sign into the gym, grab a condescendingly small towel and a glass of water and make their way towards the treadmill. They will probably stop on the way to pick up the remote control for the television, so they can commandeer the entertainment as they run, switching from the moribund generic music channel broadcast to every treadmiller's favourite viewing: Sky News.

Now, outdoor runners often look down on treadmill joggers. They point out that the treadmill belt helps leg turnover, which means you can run faster on them than you would naturally on pavement. Also, some soft tissue hardening that comes with road running does not occur when you only use treadmills.

But the treadmill terrier doesn't mind. If they are only ever going to run on treadmills, comparisons with open-air running are irrelevant. Who even cares about that? Only snotty outdoor fundamentalists, that's who!

'Well,' sniffs the outdoor runner, thinking they have found a clincher of an argument, 'have you ever considered that treadmill running cannot replicate the weather conditions of running in the park? Eh?'

Yet whenever the terrier looks out of the gym window, they don't think much of the weather conditions they see, whatever the time of year. Ice and snow in the winter, stifling heat in the summer, and rain for much of the rest of the year. What is so great about that, thinks the terrier, as they run along in the perfectly controlled temperature of the gym.

And there's another benefit for the terrier: they are always the first runner to learn of any breaking news...

Running Myths Reconsidered: You Need to Have an Athletic Body Type

Go along to any running event and you will see all physiques, from barrel-chested bounders to beany bouncers. Anyone can run.

Why Boozing Can Be Good for Running

Many of us know a boozy runner. They hit the bar straight after every training session or running event, often downing a pint of beer for every mile they've just run.

In many ways, this is a curious habit, for not only does the booze cancel out any good the run did them, but if it has been a long run – and long drinking session – it also all combines with the general fatigue and dehydration to give them a weapons-grade hangover in the morning.

Running experts say that if you must have a post-race drink, you should make sure you rehydrate thoroughly with water first. You should then just limit yourself to a maximum of two drinks. Go beyond that and you'll be messing with your recovery.

But what about a pre-run booze-up, I hear you ask. What? Surely such a thing could not exist? Well, certainly a cheeky drink the evening before a run cannot do you too much damage, provided you are restrained about it. This is a view that is upheld by Matthew Barnes, Ph.D., who studies the effects of alcohol and exercise at New Zealand's Massey University. He told Greatist that a single alcoholic beverage the night before a race is unlikely to have any impact on performance, particularly if you are a regular drinker.

But what about drinking straight before a run? That would be madness, surely? Well, not necessarily. A study published in the *Journal of Cardiovascular Medicine* found that three shots of whiskey (diluted with water) made no significant impact on treadmill runs for the 10 healthy men taking part in the study.

Perhaps there can be drink-run limits, as there are drink-drive limits for motorists. Then we could look into which boozy drinks have most carbohydrates: drinks such as beer contain the most, champagne has almost none.

Some boozing runners will have really done their homework on the health benefits of various alcoholic drinks. They could tell you that white wine contains tyrosol and caffeic acid, which reduce inflammatory reactions. Or that a pint of lager supplies one-tenth of your RDA of niacin, which pumps up your energy levels. Or why not try cider? A pint of that will give you 20 per cent of your RDA of iron, which enhances your oxygen delivery. A cheeky slurp of bitter will aid your bones and help fend off osteoporosis. A gin, on the other hand, will flush out your system, aiding kidney ailments.

What good news this all is for the boozing runner! He or she might like to toast it with a glass of champagne. And why the hell not – bubbly has a positive effect on cardiovascular ability, according to a Reading University study. Cheers, my dears!

The inspiration for boozing runners is probably a man called James Nielsen. In 2014, he broke the record for the Beer Mile — a 1-mile race in which the runner must stop every 400 metres (400 yards) to neck a beer. The record of 5:09 had been held until then by Jim Finlayson of British Columbia, but Nielsen trained for a year and smashed that record. His finish time was 4:57:1, the first sub-five-minute Beer Mile. And if that isn't laying down a challenge to boozing runners everywhere, I don't know what is. Get training, people!

Runners You Know: The Headphone Fan

For many a runner, the joy of the pursuit is to connect with nature. To feel the air against your face, the sun against your neck. The sights and the sounds. The cheeps of the birds, the barking of dogs, the conversation of people. What joy to connect, to focus outwards!

Well, this runner is different. The Headphoned Harrier wants to go deep inside himself. His headphones are about more than listening to music or recorded chatter. They are also his defensive blanket against a world he does not wish to engage with as he trots. They are the portable cave he retreats into mentally.

Of course, there are many reasons to have your own audio entertainment as you run. You cannot hear the heavy breathing of yourself or other runners. Often, hearing all that panting and puffing can make your own breathing intensify and hasten in sympathy. Before you know it, someone else's exhausted heavy breathing has dragged you into a vortex of over-breathy fatigue.

There is also the massive motivation that recorded music or chat can bring. Many runners have 'power songs' they can flick to mid-run, tunes that give them an injection of energy just when they need it. Songs such as 'Simply The Best' by Tina Turner and the theme from the Rocky films feature prominently. But really, music of any sort can distract you during activities. Who knows how many miles music can add to your threshold?

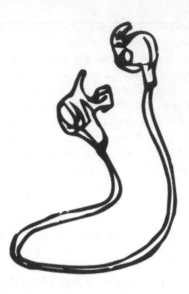

Chat, too, can be a brilliant boost. Download an audiobook and get lost in the plot as you run. The story can drown out that voice that comes and tells you you're too tired to carry on. Podcasts are also an excellent and welcome addition to the auditory menu. Free of charge, you have trillions of hours of chat at your fingertips, on any topic you like.

So the Headphoned Harrier is to be empathised with – but not by all. Some runners look with disdain at their ear-plugged comrades, feeling somehow personally snubbed by their headphones. Event organisers, too, have often taken against headphones, issuing safety guidelines discouraging their use, or even banning them altogether from events, and disqualifying any runner who defies the ban.

But as any headphone fan will tell you, when you are in the full flow of running, and your favourite song suddenly comes on, you can reach a point of such multi-sensory elevation that you will feel you have gone to heaven.

Long may we plug in as we push away. Just don't forget to charge the music device's battery before you set out...

Remember...

Pace is relative. What you describe as a steady pace might feel like lung-busting, breakneck speed to someone else. But before you get too smug about it, remember that what is an easy pace to someone else might be unbearably fast to you. The same is true of distance: merely telling someone you are planning a 'long' run is irrelevant unless you tell them the distance.

Why do all the cute ones RUN away?

Funny Spectator Signs at Running Events

You Can Tell a Lot by How Someone Runs...

It is sometimes said that you can learn much about an individual's temperament by giving them an online task to do on a computer with an excruciatingly slow internet connection.

Similarly, some employers interview job candidates in restaurants, so they can gauge their personality by how they treat waiting staff.

But you can actually tell a lot about a person by observing how they run. Do they run with grace, patience or flow? Or are they erratic, tetchy and perilous?

For instance, if you wanted to choose someone to drive your children to school, you could do worse than watch how they run. If they are distracted and unaware of their surroundings, it might be best to politely decline their offer of a lift.

Then there is the honesty factor: we have all spotted people who cut corners at parkrun and other events. It's not the biggest crime in the universe, but it is a telling glimpse into their personality.

Equally, you can see how determined and persistent people are when they run. As their body tires, the wind begins to blow against them, and there is every reason to slow down or give up, does the runner wave the white flag? Or do they grit their teeth and plough on, resolute in their intention to complete the task?

The latter runner is the one you want in your life. So take a look at people as they run.

Weird Marathons:
Walt Disney World Marathon

Billed, perhaps inevitably, as 'the most magical race on earth', this 26-miler takes in four Walt Disney World theme parks, including Magic Kingdom and Disney's Hollywood Studios. Perfect for the big kid, and something of a no-brainer for the entertainment giant's merchandisers, the route is lined by Disney characters and other distractions. At the end, the sweaty runners are presented with a Mickey Mouse Finisher Medal.

Running Philosophy

66 Running was the thing I could do on my own, with no one to compete against. It cleared my head and stopped me from going bonkers when I was getting up at 4 a.m. to present a breakfast show, with all the myopic egotism that can create. **99**

Sian Williams, TV presenter

Notable Runners: Kathrine Switzer

Women used to be banned from being registered runners at the Boston Marathon but Switzer managed to get a number. As she ran the 26.2 miles, a race official tried to bundle her off the course, but her boyfriend helped her fend off the man. She went on to also win the NYC Marathon in 1974.

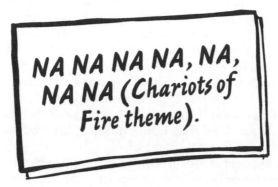

Funny Spectator Signs at Running Events

Remember...

When people running at an event in which you are also participating are much slower than you, remember that you, too, were a beginner once. It's likely that anyone moving at a gradual pace is in their early days of running. This might be the first event they've taken part in and your attitude to them might make or break whether or not they become lifetime runners. So don't run perilously close behind, huffing and puffing in the hope they will speed up or get out of your way. And definitely don't elbow past them.

Runners You Know: The Addict

Alcoholics Anonymous and other abstinence-based recovery methods are based on a 12-step programme. But for the running addict, the main problem is not doing as many as 12 steps, but reducing their step output to anywhere near such a small number.

Running offers a whole load of emotional benefits – it releases a glorious cocktail of the pain-relievers endorphins and dopamine, the anti-depressant serotonin, and other goodies. This joyful stuff flows through you as you run, anchoring the experience with feeling good. No wonder people get hooked.

For running addicts, withdrawal leads to a come-down punctuated by depression, apathy and listlessness. Many runners also find that as they become more dependent on their exercise, that a 'tolerance level' kicks in, meaning they have to run further and further to achieve the same effect.

In 2009, scientists at Tufts University in Massachusetts, USA, lead by Professor Robin Kanarek reported that: 'excessive running shares similarities with drug-taking behaviour'. Writing in the medical journal *Behavioral Neuroscience*, they said that too much running causes a reaction in the brain that is similar to heroin – and it is just as addictive.

'Although exercise is good for your health, extreme exercise may be physically addictive,' they concluded. The running addict can relate.

Worried that you know a running addict, or that you might even be one yourself?

Here are some dead-giveaway warning signs to look out for:

1. The addict will continue to run even when they are unwell or injured. They could be battling weapons-grade influenza as the nation shivers through the iciest of snaps and still they'll show up at the starting line.
2. An injured leg is seen not as a reason to rest but, if anything, a reason to run. 'I reckon a swift 10k will run off the injury,' says the addict. Even if they have to set off like a ghoulish, wounded extra from the *Thriller* video, they simply cannot miss a run.

3. They are in spectacular denial. This means they regularly refute out loud that they are addicted to running, even when no one has suggested they are. Interesting.
4. Every so often they embark on an entirely random and spontaneous run. They might be out walking with the family, clothed in everyday civilian garb including non-training shoes, when they suddenly take off on a cheeky sprint. They may not even realise themselves that they are doing it.
5. They subscribe to every running magazine going. They listen to podcasts about running while they are out running. They type 'running' into Google News several times a day. They even buy books about running, obsessively. (But they shouldn't really worry too much about that aspect. It seems a good idea to me.)
6. Unlike other runners who become obsessed with weather forecasts and apps, they scarcely even notice what running conditions are like. To them, a sweet, sunny spring day is no different to the freezing pits of winter or the dankest doldrums of autumn. The fact is that there is an outdoors and it is there to be run through.
7. They pick up injuries nearly as often as they collect medals. When, inevitably, they get an injury so serious that they physically cannot run, they stagger around the local swimming pool, determined not to lose form. When they are out on the streets and they see other runners, they are so angry and envious they want to kill them.

What will become of the running addict? Perhaps they only have one hope: a 12-step recovery programme:

'Hi, I'm Bob, and I'm a runnerholic.'

'Hi Bob...'

Good luck, guys. One day at a time...

My Running Story:
Dr. Philip Clarke

It is a well-known fact that regular exercise has a wide range of positive implications on both our physical and mental health. Today, it is common to see in every town, city or village people out on the roads running, and within this section I want to talk about the impact this form of exercise can have on our emotional health and well-being.

For many people, distance running is an opportunity to make sense of their trials and tribulations, and allows freedom and time to come up with potential solutions for these. In doing so, it can help people make sense of the situation and cope more effectively, mentally and emotionally, helped by the increased endorphins released in the brain when partaking in exercise. These endorphins are commonly known as one of the 'happy chemicals' released in the brain after exercise.

This is supported by research, which proposes that running is an effective tool to aid individuals with weathering emotional stress (Salmon, 2001; Bernstein and McNally, 2017). We as humans love to feel in control of our life and events, so it is little wonder that stress predominately stems from uncontrollable sources, such as financial, family, work or relationship issues.

Running provides an opportunity for the individual to regain control, since they can dictate the pace, distance and direction of their run, meaning they can push themselves harder as a way of venting or releasing these negative emotions. Furthermore, in recent studies, research has revealed that exercise helps reduce symptoms of Post-Traumatic Stress Disorder (PTSD) after just two weeks (Fetzner and Asmundson, 2015) and demonstrated sustained benefits after a prolonged period of exercise of 12 weeks (Rosenbaum, Sherrington and Tiedemann, 2015).

Research has also shown that after even just 30 minutes of aerobic exercise (such as long-distance running) individuals are better able to regulate their emotions and be more positive in light of challenging situations (Bernstein and McNally, 2017).

This further highlights the positive impact that regular exercise, such as running, can have on our ability to regulate our emotions and improve our overall emotional well-being.

Emotion can also be a great vehicle for change in our exercise patterns and help motivate us to achieve things that we may have felt we were unable to do. For instance, the number of people completing marathons, half marathons and fun runs is on the rise, with the main driving force of this being the emotional connection with the charity an individual does the event for. The power of the 'why' someone does something, and the emotional connection of it, can lead to people being more resilient and mentally tough in the face of adversity – for example, when hitting the wall in a marathon, or pushing through those last few miles of training.

The power of the emotional 'why' is something I personally have experienced. In 2010, I was doing my Masters degree in Sport and Exercise Psychology in Wales. I came back to Ireland for Christmas and I found out my mother had been diagnosed with brain cancer at the age of 49. Like anyone, this was something that hit me hard, and I wanted to stay at home to help my mother with her rehabilitation. However, my mother disagreed, and ensured I went back to Wales to continue with my education. This was something I found very difficult and struggled to cope with.

I wanted to do something to support my mother, so I decided I would run the length of Ireland for the local cancer charity that was helping to support her. This task was made even more challenging since I had never taken part in any long-distance running prior to this, not even a 5k. With the support of one of my close friends, whose mother had passed away from cancer at a young age, we decided to both undertake this challenge and do it for our mothers.

Five months later, we crossed the finish line in Malin Head in Donegal after running 671 kilometres (417 miles) over 13 consecutive days. The motivation and drive I felt in that five-month period was unlike anything I had ever experienced, and it was all down to knowing my 'why', and the emotional impact of this. Whenever I was struggling during a run or to get up at 5 a.m.

to go out and run in the cold or rain, that 'why' was far more powerful than the 'how' I was going to achieve it. This enabled me to just put one foot in front of the other and just keep repeating the action when the going was tough.

It wasn't until afterwards that I truly understood that this event, and all the running I had done, not only helped raise money for charity, but it also helped me cope with the most difficult time of my life, and if it weren't for that emotional drive, I am not sure I would have been able to go from couch to 16 marathons in 13 days.

Dr Philip Clarke is a lecturer in Sport and Exercise Psychology at the University of Derby, England.

Remember...

Running on the beach is overrated. I mean, sure, it seems like the ultimate romantic running experience when you imagine it from your home, hundreds of miles from the nearest shoreline. But when you get there you realise that, novel as the experience is, it is also very problematic. The surface is all over the place, there is rubbish sticking out of the sand, and the whole place just smells a bit dodgy. Like barbeques and picnics, beach running is something that seems great in your head but generally lets you down.

Things We Hate About Running: The Loos

The loos at running events are enough to turn the stomach of the hardiest of harriers. By the time queues of nervous runners have done their absolute worst in these cramped chambers, they have become repellent places to be. But it's not as if you are going to 'bake it' until the end of the half marathon, so you've little choice but to hold your nose, avert your gaze as much as is possible, and get in and out as quickly as you can.

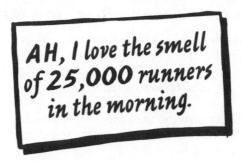

AH, I love the smell of 25,000 runners in the morning.

Funny Spectator Signs at Running Events

Running Myths Reconsidered: You Must Drink at Every Water Station

Experts have argued for ages about whether you should allow thirst to be your guide during running events. Some say that if you wait until you are thirsty then you are already dehydrated. Others point out that drinking regardless of what your body is telling you risks stomach upsets and over-hydration. See what works best for you.

Runners You Know: The Fun Runner

If there's a charity 5k anywhere near the fun runner's house, they will be there on the day, full of jolly enthusiasm for the event. In the old days, they would spend the weeks leading up to the event wielding a clipboard and pen, collecting sponsorships for the cause. Nowadays they have moved the begging online.

Although fun runners are sometimes regarded with mild disapproval by more serious folk, their very name tells you all you really need to know: they are all about the fun. And since when has that been anything but a good thing?

A Brisk Guide to the New York Marathon

The inaugural New York City Marathon was held in 1970. The entry fee was $1.

This event featured just 127 entrants running four laps around Central Park. By 2015 it boasted rather more runners: 50,000 of them.

For that debut marathon not everyone completed the course. In fact, just 55 men lasted the 26.2 miles, and the sole female runner dropped out due to illness.

The winner, Gary Muhrcke, had put in an evening shift as a firefighter the night before the race. He was so tired on the morning of the marathon that he told his wife he would drop out. However, she convinced him to do it and the rest is history.

In 1972, the six female runners were told by the sport's governing body that they would be given a 10-minute head start. However, deeming this unfair, they sat down in protest against the policy, waving banners bearing slogans such as: 'Hey, this is 1972. Wake up.' They then started with everyone else.

Until 1976, the marathon was run entirely within the boundaries of Central Park. After being re-routed that year to mark the US Bicentennial, the path has snaked its way through five boroughs ever since.

The following year, an eight-year-old boy became the youngest ever finisher. Wesley Paul from Columbia, Missouri managed to complete the course in a phenomenal 3:00:37. The minimum age for runners is now 18, so Wesley's record is unlikely to be bettered any time soon.

Like a bit of pasta? What about a lot of pasta? The official Marathon Eve Dinner, which is hosted by New York Road Runners, serves up 2270kg (5000lb) of wholewheat pasta and 2.25 metric tons of rigatoni. An Atkins dieter's worst nightmare.

More than 2.5 million spectators line the course, which goes through Staten Island, Brooklyn, Queens, the Bronx and Manhattan.

The race is started with the sound of a canon and the playing of Frank Sinatra's classic track 'New York, New York' over the PA system.

In 1994, Mexican elite runner Germán Silva was in the lead when he made a wrong turn during the final mile. He was supposed to continue west to Columbus Circle, but turned into Central Park instead. Realising his mistake, he turned around and chased down Benjamín Paredes, who had taken the lead. Silva still won with a time of 2:11:21.

The route is fastest as it passes through Brooklyn. The mostly flat terrain produces an average speed of 5:08 minutes per kilometre (8:14 minutes per mile).

The Queensboro Bridge is considered one of the most challenging parts of the course. Coming around the 16th mile, it is steep, and with spectators banned from the bridge there is no one to encourage you across.

In 1986, Vietnam veteran Bob Weiland crossed the finish line in 4 days, 2 hours, 47 minutes and 17 seconds, having tackled the entire route on his hands. He had lost his legs in battle 17 years earlier.

In 1993, a couple from Chicago stopped at mile eight to tie the knot. Tom Young donned a top hat and tuxedo while his girlfriend Pam Kezios, 31, stepped into a white dress to exchange vows. After the ceremony, they continued with the race.

Water stations through the course are stocked with 62,370 gallons of water and 32,040 gallons of Gatorade. Some 2.3 million paper cups are typically used.

The event was cancelled in 2012 after Hurricane Sandy battered part of the course. Some disappointed entrants assembled in Central Park to run their own unsanctioned race, while others decided to travel to Staten Island to support recovery efforts.

Studies showed that the average NYC Marathon finisher runs 55 kilometres (34 miles) per week during training.

In 2000, the race included an official wheelchair division for the first time.

Rapper Sean 'P. Diddy' Combs ran the 2003 Marathon. During training, he gave up sex for two weeks. 'I'm abstaining from sex,' he said. 'My hormones are raging ... but it's for the kids.' He was running on behalf of three children's charities and raised $2 million.

In 2008 there were three deaths. Carlos Jose Gomes, 58, of Brazil fell unconscious after completing the race in 4:12:15. An autopsy revealed he had a pre-existing heart condition. Staten Island's Joseph Marotta, 66, also died of a heart attack hours after the event, and Fred Costa, 41, from Cincinnati, Ohio, collapsed at the marathon and passed away several days later from a heart attack.

In 2013, charity volunteers collected 26 tonnes of clothing that had been abandoned by runners during the run. Most of this was dumped in the first 3 kilometres (2 miles).

Here's a curious record for you: in 2014, David Babcock, a professor at the University of Central Missouri, broke the Guinness World Record for the longest scarf knitted while running a marathon.

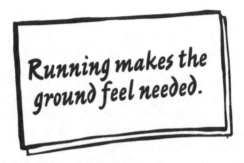

Running makes the ground feel needed.

Funny Spectator Signs at Running Events

Things We Hate About Running: Smelly Runners

These fall into three camps: those who arrive clean as a whistle and liberally sprayed with loud deodorant, attacking aftershave or pompous perfume; those who arrive un-bathed and in sweaty kit; and those who break wind ad lib as you are all squeezed in the starting pen. Thanks, people.

Remember...

You will always look awful in race photos. As you run, in your head, you might be a bronzed beauty or an athletic hunk, all that sweat and toil transforming you into a better physical specimen. After all, running dozens of miles each week must make you stunning, right? Well, the race photographer will certainly bring you crashing down to earth.

Whether the photographer snaps you 35 kilometres (22 miles) into a marathon or 200 metres (200 yards) into your parkrun, the one certainty is that you will look terrible. Your face will be contorted like that of an extra in a nuclear war film, your awkward posture will ensure that your body looks its worst, rather than its best, and you might even have a bit of drool emerging from your mouth, or a drop of snot poking out of your beak.

It's just one of the rules of running: the race photographer will make you look less healthy than a burger-guzzling fatso on the sidelines. The camera never lies, they say. Well, at running events it absolutely fibs through its teeth – the swine!

Running Philosophy

❝ I have always felt strongly about introducing the benefits of sports to children and others. Running has brought me such a great deal as a person, and I want others to share this feeling. **❞**

Paula Radcliffe, MBE, world record-holder
for women's marathon

Weird Marathons:
Great Wall Marathon

This annual event in the Tianjin Province of China includes long sections through the lower valley and the villages. However, the real drama comes during the 6 kilometres (3.7 miles) of the route on the Great Wall itself. Here, the runner is faced by more than 5000 leg-demolishing stone steps, and arduous ascents and descents, including a notorious 'Goat Track'. The route includes phenomenal views but many runners are too busy trying to not 'hit the Great Wall' to appreciate them.

How to Not Become a Running Bore

Running is such an exciting hobby to get involved in that you sometimes feel like telling the whole world all about it. After all, your progress as a runner is endlessly fascinating to you. So why can't it be fascinating, or at least reasonably interesting, to everyone else? Well, the danger is that you might become a running bore, who chews the ears off everyone in your vicinity with hellishly detailed, blow-by-blow accounts of your latest jogging escapades.

But at the same time, running is your hobby and passion. So it should not be entirely off limits. The question is: how do you find a happy balance? Here are a few broad guidelines to stick to:

Marathons

It's cool to say you have run one and to mention your finishing time. It's not cool to go into such detail that you speak about the 26.2 miles for nearly as long as you spent running them.

Parkrun

Tell people about the marvellous community spirit that these free, timed runs foster.

Don't tell people about the intricacies of your quest to beat your PB, including attempts at interval running, fast starts, sprinted finishes, split analysis, etc...

Training

It's fine to give people a basic overview of the many joys and benefits of running, perhaps tailoring the information so it appeals to the individual you're speaking with and their life.

It's not fine to give people so much detail that they feel as breathless, sweaty and exhausted as they would if they tackled a marathon from scratch.

Weight loss

Do tell them that running will help them to lose weight reasonably effortlessly.

Don't make out that weight loss is the only reason anyone runs, or that it is a good idea to be primarily motivated by it.

Medals

Don't show people your medals unless they specifically ask to see them, without any prompting from you. Otherwise, it's just wrong to show them your medals. How wrong? Well, unsolicited showing of medals is, in truth, scarcely more polite than unsolicited showing of faecal stools. Does that help clear it up?

In short

Do tell people that running is easy and fun (because it is).

Don't tell people that running is tough and challenging (because you think that makes you, as a runner, seem more impressive.)

Things People Shout at Runners

Runners You Know: The Over-Dresser

After putting on their running T-shirt and shorts, they climb into their heavy, padded tracksuits and slip into their Antarctic socks. They then tie an extra sweater around their waist, before donning gloves and a woollen hat. Maybe a scarf, too. 'I am just going outside and may be some time,' they think, taking a deep breath. It's the middle of July.

The over-dresser is blissfully unaware of the first rule of running clothing: dress for how warm you'll feel 10 minutes into the run. Instead, they emerge for a 5-kilometre (3-mile) jog looking like they're headed for a heroic, perilous expedition across the North Pole.

Whether it's aversion to cold, a fear that the weather might suddenly turn halfway through a short run, or self-consciousness about their bodies, these people layer themselves up like bulging onions, surely adding many, many minutes to their completion time.

They nearly always look absolutely shattered when they cross the finishing line. But then so would you if you had a full department store of clobber on your back as you huffed and puffed around the local park.

Sleep Well

Just as you should carb-load before long race events, you should also kip load. According to research by the journal *Medicine & Science In Sports & Exercise*, getting some extra sleep in ahead of the big day can help you towards a faster finish time. The study found that sleeping for an extra 75 minutes on six consecutive nights will bring increased endurance and a lower perception of exertion. Interestingly, this held true even for those runners who, the evening before the event, had disrupted sleep, or even no sleep, due to nerves.

My Running Story:
Author and Cartoonist Russell Taylor

Just over a year ago, at the age of 55, I was diagnosed with lymphatic cancer. It came up in a routine blood test – I didn't have any symptoms, and didn't even feel particularly unwell. To be told completely out of the blue that I had a life-threatening illness was not only strange, surreal and scary, but it also seemed profoundly unfair. The causes of lymphoma are unknown, so there was nothing in my lifestyle I could blame it on. On the contrary, as a vegetarian and dedicated runner and cyclist I theoretically belonged to a low-risk group. Unlike many of my carnivorous couch-potato contemporaries I had been sensible and responsible in my life, yet I was the one who was now in danger of losing it.

So it was that despite feeling perfectly healthy I found myself at the end of last year embarking on a six-month course of chemotherapy. The drug used to treat my type of lymphoma (non-Hodgkin, as you ask) is Bendamustine, which is a derivative of mustard gas. On the 100th anniversary of the Battle of the Somme I was lying on a bed in the Whittington Hospital in North London, England, having this celebrated poison drip-fed into my veins. It's always nice to know that life has a sense of humour.

The unlikely remedy proved remarkably effective and a PET scan in January revealed that the cancer had gone. I was in 100 per cent remission. It is due to just such a chance of complete recovery that those in the know reckon lymphoma is the cancer of choice to get (though obviously it's better just not to get cancer in the first place). It responds very well to treatment. The only problem is that, like a villain in a 1980s' Hollywood movie, it has a nasty habit of coming back again.

So, having obtained the All Clear, my mission was now to keep the cancer at bay for as long as possible. I did a bit of reading and found that to have the best chance of long-term survival there are three principles to observe. First, maintain a positive mental attitude. Check. Second, follow a good diet. Check. And, third, take regular exercise. Ah...

I realised that I hadn't put on my running shoes or got on my bike for a year. Even though I had been pretty much free of symptoms or side effects from either the cancer or the chemo, somehow I'd been thinking of myself as an invalid and had given myself an 'off PE' note. The problem is that once you've got out of the habit of exercising it is strangely hard to get back into. Even when I knew that it could literally be a matter of life or death for me I still found myself procrastinating and making excuses not to climb out of bed and go for a run.

Then one morning in February (when I was sitting at my computer rather than slogging round the park) I got an email out of the blue from a person I didn't know with the rather exotic name of Chas Newkey-Burden. He informed me he was writing a book on running and asked me for a contribution. Since there was no payment involved he resorted to a cunning strategy: lavishly praising a book I had written 15 years ago on marathon running (*The Looniness of the Long Distance Runner*, Andre Deutsch Ltd, 2001). He also promised to invite me to the launch party for his book. Flattery and freebies: that's a combination you can't go wrong with when you're trying to get a writer to do something for you.

But there was another even more persuasive reason for me to accept this unsolicited gig. It gave me a deadline. Not that literal Deadline of Death, which hangs over all of us and really ought to have been my motivation to get down to some training, but a much milder deadline: that someone whom I'd never even met would get cross with me if I failed to deliver a piece for him. And in order to write the piece I would have to start running again.

Creativity and exercise might seem to be two totally opposed activities – one static and cerebral, the other active and physical – but they are actually directly linked. Running releases beta-Endorphin into the brain, which stimulates creative thinking. I wrote most of my marathon book on a dictation machine that I used to carry in my pocket whenever I went running. I swear I could have achieved a better time at the New York City Marathon in 1999 if I hadn't been slowing down every five minutes to record thoughts and observations that had occurred to me.

So, I find that this unexpected, unremunerated commission from a total stranger has finally given me the incentive I was looking for to lace up my trainers and head off to run round the park. Now I just need to work out what on earth I'm going to write about.

Russell Taylor MBE is half of the creative team that produces the Alex *cartoon strip in the* Daily Telegraph. *His book on marathon running,* The Looniness of the Long Distance Runner, *is available on Amazon.*

Things We Hate About Running: Brain Loops on Long Runs

'So, that's 10 miles done ... right, if I do 9-minute miles then that's 10 x 9 but then there'll be 11, be weird if that was in kilometres, so that's 10 x 6 because that's a 10k if...'

RUN like millennials, RUN from commitment!

Funny Spectator Signs at Running Events

Remember...

A good method of keeping your torso, neck and head relaxed as you run is to pretend you are holding a potato chip in each hand. Imagine that you do not want to drop the chips or crush them. These leave your fingers lightly curled with your thumbs resting on top, promoting a relaxed arm action, which benefits the arms and shoulders. Better a chip in your hand than a chip on your shoulder, you could say. Some runners find a good way of getting this right is to imagine they are going to eat the chips at the end of the run.

Run Like a Girl

Female runners have to contend with various factors that boys don't: namely, hormones, being pregnant, and boobs. Each of these poses its own particular problem, something that reluctant runners will seize upon as excuses for not putting on their trainers and getting out there.

The fact is, though, that running is generally beneficial when it comes to easing the symptoms of menstrual pains and mood swings, and being fit and healthy is definitely a boon when you are in labour. And you can just buy a really good sports bra to sort out your bosom.

Moreover, a US study quoted in *Runner's World* found that running women produce a less potent form of oestrogen than their inactive equivalents. This means that female runners slash by half their risks of developing breast and uterine cancer, and by two-thirds their risk of contracting a common form of diabetes. Pretty impressive.

Once pregnant, female runners do have to accept that their bodies are different, and should always seek professional medical advice specific to them and their level of fitness rather than relying on sometimes controversial and contradictory information on the internet. That said, in general, experts say running should cause no problems in the first trimester and most runners will be OK during the second trimester, though running in the final three months of pregnancy is generally discouraged. The key thing for a pregnant runner is to avoid becoming overheated, as a core body temperature above 38.3°C (101°F) could increase the risk of birth defects.

Did you Know?

One in 75,100 – the American College of Cardiology's calculation of the risk of suffering a heart attack during a marathon.

Running Myths Reconsidered:
Eating Bananas Prevents Cramping

It is often said that cramping is caused by a lack of potassium. However, exercise psychologist Tim Noakes, who wrote the book *The Lore of Running* (Human Kinetics, 1985), says cramps are more down to muscle fatigue, dehydration and poor preparation.

Running Philosophy

" We all have had injuries and disappointments. It is a part of running. It can bring us down and at times be overwhelming when we see how far we have to go. But I encourage you all to take your time, stay inspired **"** and focused.

Kara Goucher, Olympic distance runner

Remember…

A really good way to make a run seem longer and more tiring is to check your watch every few minutes. Try it – it works!

Runners You Know:
The Kamikaze Runner

To describe this type of runner as enthusiastic would be an understatement. Like a pumped-up cheetah who has sunk a vat of coffee, you always absolutely pelt it as you run.

With minimal spatial awareness, you hardly notice as more measured runners abruptly fling themselves out of your suicidal, exuberant path.

You are loosely related to the big finishers at 5ks and 10ks, who deliberately leave some 'fuel in the tank' for the end of the race, and, as they near the finishing line break into a gallop, haughtily shouting: 'Coming through ... coming through ... I SAID COMING THROUGH!!!'

The main difference is that in your case you probably won't shout such a warning. Your path is your path regardless of obstacles, and not even a child in your way is going to slow you down. They will have to move aside or face the consequences.

So, dear reader, if you see a kamikaze runner coming your way, the best thing is to be the bigger person and leap out of the way, rather than insisting on standing your ground. No one wants to get flattened.

You're not SLOW, you're getting your MONEY'S worth.

Funny Spectator Signs at Running Events

Weird Marathons: North Pole Marathon

Once you've decided you want to run a marathon, you are faced with the decision of where to run it. London or New York, for instance. Or even the North Pole. Although you may not feel like it, you'll be on top of the world as you negotiate 26.2 miles of Arctic ice floes and hard snow in sub-zero temperatures. Keep an eye out for polar bears, though. This is perfect for the frustrated Arctic adventurer. In 2015, just 47 people were brave/silly enough to take on this challenge.

Get your knees up!

Things People Shout at Runners

Runners You Know: The Gadget Guru

When gadget gurus line up for a race, they aren't just warming up, stretching their muscles, or quietly focusing their minds on the challenge ahead. They are fiddling with their phones, groping their GPS monitors, and setting their sports watches. As the starting pistol sounds, you can hear the beeps and squeaks of their various bits of equipment, and you can identify them easily – the runners who look a bit like the bionic man.

With at least four smartphone apps open and their body strapped with everything from heart-rate monitors to activity trackers, they set off on the run looking like something from a futuristic sci-fi film. All this gadgetry and technology won't so much analyse their run as systematically scrutinise it like a hi-tech stalker.

After running all morning, gadget gurus will spend the afternoon at their computer, downloading data and graphs. They then document their latest run in gruesome detail across

Facebook, Twitter and other social networks, all to the yawning indifference of their followers and friends. [See also: 'The Social Media Bore' on page 32.]

But who cares what other people think? Modern technology is a treasure chest of intrigue for the runner, and following the minutiae of their progress keeps gadget gurus motivated all year round.

A love of gadgetry also paves the way for regular shopping, as new apps, software and hardware come on the market. Who doesn't like an excuse for a bit of retail therapy?

Moreover, when a gadget-less, technophobe runner approaches them at an event to see if they can help them work out their pace, gadget gurus bask in the satisfaction that they are providing a public service.

What better time has there been to be a gadget guru? Technology is accelerating like a short-distance sprinter: just the other day, one heard that some runners buy drones to follow them around on their training runs. What a colossal waste of money. It would be crazy not to get one.

Signs You Have Run Too Hard

1. When you are out running you feel like you are running through water.
2. As you crash out on the sofa after your run, the phone rings and you attempt to answer your banana. Or your shoe.
4. While assembling a post-run stir-fry, you reach for the soy sauce, only to absent-mindedly sprinkle liquid plant food all over your noodles and tofu. It doesn't taste too bad. You only realise the next day, when all your plants have died because of the soy sauce/water combination you fed them with the previous night.
5. You're so stroppy that discussions with your spouse over what to have for dinner are conducted with the sort of passion and bitterness usually reserved for debates about fox hunting, capital punishment or religion.
6. Sleep? Sleep is just a myth!
7. Your resting heart rate rises as your nervous system releases extra hormones that speed up your heart to move more oxygen to the muscles and brain.
8. You cannot – *really* cannot – get out of your post-run bath.
9. Your legs feel sore for days at a time.
10. Your urine is dark yellow. Or even borderline brown. Ewww.
11. You keep craving sugar. Where's the sugar? Give me more sugar!
12. I'm thirsty. Is anyone else thirsty? I'm thirsty. I might just have another drink...
13. A throbbing headache.
14. You keep taking offence at things.
15. You're tired.

My Running Story:
Political Strategist Alastair Campbell

A lot of people focus on what running can do for the body. I've always been more interested in what it can do for the mind.

For a start, running has really helped me write books and speeches. In *What I Talk About When I Talk About Running* (Random House USA, 2009), Haruki Murakami writes: 'Most of what I know about writing I've learned through running every day.'

I can relate. Writing and running have several parallels. They also call on similar qualities, such as focus and endurance. For me, a disappointing run is one during which I do not have an idea good enough to text to myself so that I can follow it up when I get home.

In fact, for many years, my solution to any kind of mental block has been to go for a run, with my BlackBerry in pocket, ready to record whatever emerges as the miles gently ease aside the mental blocks.

When I was working in Downing Street I took to running to and from work most days – amounting to about 13 kilometres (8 miles) every working day. These runs really cleared my head – the more important things started to sort themselves out in my mind, and I let go of the less important things.

Pounding the pavement also helped me deal with depression. I began to find that as I ran my mind would go to a completely different place. I'd find myself several kilometres/miles into a run and have no idea how I'd got there, because my mind had simply taken off.

On other days it can be more of a struggle, but there are mental tricks you can use to keep yourself going. If I'm feeling a bit down when I go out for a run, I sometimes decide to run to the next lamp post and then the next car, and so on. Before you know it, you've covered the distance.

Everyday running can give you these little boosts, but the most dramatic mental moment comes when you cross the finishing line at a marathon. Then you experience one of the greatest emotional highs of your life. Bask in it.

Alastair Campbell is a writer, communicator and strategist best known for his role as former British Prime Minister Tony Blair's spokesman, press secretary and director of communications and strategy. He is also the author of several books, including Winners: And How They Succeed *(Arrow, 2016), a number-one best-selling analysis of what it takes to win in politics, business and sport.*

Did you Know?

Thirty per cent – the increase in sex that 78 people who began running four times a week reported for a study at the University of California, San Diego.

Funny Spectator Signs at Running Events

Runners You Know: Mr Saddlebags

You redecorate your T-shirt with sweat within the first half-kilometre, you salty devil!

What Your Favourite Distance
Says About You

The 5k

You enjoy running but you also want to get on with the rest of your life. You might well be married to someone who doesn't approve of your hobby. Some might say you are the athletic equivalent of the reveller in the bar who leaves after one drink.

The 10k

You fancy the glory of a longer-sounding distance without the gruelling demands that an actual long distance brings. You sometimes silently debate which sounds longer: 10k or 6.2 miles. But with its balance of speed and length, this distance is a great choice for the level-headed.

The 10-miler

Woooaaah there, aren't you the edgy one, slipping outside of the popular running distances? When you tried half marathons you found the training too demanding, but you think the 10k sounds a bit limp. So you settled for the 10-miler and you're pretty happy with your decision ... but also slightly confused as to why more people aren't impressed by it.

The half marathon

Neither one thing nor the other, you are middle of the road in everything. You buy one CD a year, and it's usually a compilation. Because you can see both sides in every political issue, you haven't expressed an opinion since 1987. When you are on your deathbed, your final words will be: 'Well, it's all swings and roundabouts, isn't it?'

The marathon

You like to brag. In every conversation you are poised for opportunities to mention your achievements. If you are clever, you will open an online fundraising page, so you get to be an altruistic hero, rather than a mere hero.

The muddy run

You've got issues, possibly dating back to the potty.

The ultramarathon

You like running and you want to hide from the rest of your life. You might well be married to someone you don't really like. Some might say you are the athletic equivalent of the reveller in the bar who ends the evening in casualty.

Running for the Sake of It

With all the talk of events, personal bests and weight loss, it can be easy to lose sight of the simple joys of running for the sake of it. Leave your running watch at home, don't tell any club mates that you're heading out, and empty your mind of thoughts of pace or calorie. Just get out there, put one foot in front of another – and run.

The wind is in your face, you can feel the earth underneath your feet, and your every step takes you more into the moment. All we have is the present moment, and running can lock us right into it, shrugging off regrets and fears.

The sound of your breath unites you with other creatures who run, and the birds are producing a sweet soundtrack for you from the branches of the trees you pass. It's beautiful, isn't it?

Why do you do it to yourself, non-runners sometimes ask us? It is hard to answer in words, we can perhaps respond best by pointing at children at play. At their happiest, kids run and run. Although as adults we are encouraged to leave behind such spontaneous joy, it seems that some of us didn't get the memo – and hallelujah for that.

Life is a gift and the best thank-you letter we can write is to live. When are we more alive than while we run?

So carry on your run, and be proud of your glow. You're not running with a dehumanising number pinned to your T-shirt. You're not running for a fast time, or firmer body. There is no competition here, instead there is the most profound sense of unity with all.

You're running for the sake of it. You're running because you can.

Running Philosophy

❝ When I'm at the gym, I think about chicks, going to the beach, and looking good. I do it for the girls. **❞**

Usain Bolt, the world's fastest human and holder of more records than can be listed here...

Things We Hate About Running:
Arm-in-Arm Novelty Runners

You're all dressed up as emus or something. This is your first and only running event. You're doing the run for a charity. All of this is fine and you are quite right to be almost giddy with excitement. I hope you have a lovely day. But do you really have to link arms and jog along four abreast, blocking the paths of other runners behind you? (This menace is worsened by the fact that spectators are quite naturally much more excited and admiring of these types of runners than they are the more everyday variety, which means they encourage them to keep up the theatre all the way round.)

Runners You Know:
The Weekend Warrior

Many runners spread their weekly mileage out over four or more outings. Each week they'll do one long run, a medium-length outing, and a couple of short bursts.

The weekend warrior is the opposite. Between Monday and Friday the only way this runner is going to break a sweat is if his or her house catches fire, or they're late for a train, or if they get chased by an angry lion who has just escaped from a local zoo.

Short of such scenarios taking place, this runner will be sedentary during the weekdays. Come Saturday morning, though, the trainers, shorts and T-shirts come out of their cupboard, and the weekend warrior hits the pavements.

Like the athletic equivalent of a binge boozer, the weekend warrior will distil every inch of their weekly mileage into one colossal Saturday blowout. This will be an epic affair, in which the runner bursts through park after park, possibly even through several districts, before returning home, slumping in a chair, and vowing to avoid running for the next seven days.

These are the running world's equivalents of those who tend to their garden all weekend but never so much as look at it for the rest of the week. Or the gym members who possibly can't quite conceptualise that the gym is even open between Monday and Friday.

For years, these runners were sneered at by some in the athletic community. They were seen as undedicated part-timers, fair-weather slackers who would reap no benefits from their approach to running.

However, the weekend warrior may just have the last laugh. A study published by Loughborough University in 2017 found that exercising just once or twice a week in middle-age reduces considerably the risk of an early death. Weekend warriors, it discovered, reduce their risk of dying from any cause by 30 per cent, while those who go for a jog every day or so only reap an extra 5 per cent benefit. Given that the researchers studied 63,000 adults between 1994 and 2012, their results are worth heeding.

So, let's raise a glass to the weekend warrior. Some lifestyles simply don't allow for daily activity. And if their spasmodic approach to jogging is actually doing them a whole lot of good, who are we to judge?

Remember...

People say you should replace your running shoes after 800 kilometres (500 miles)... but people who work in running stores will sometimes try and convince you '800' should be closer to '8'. There's a reason for that.

Things People Shout at Runners

My Running Story: Author Phil Hewitt

Running is the way runners make sense of the world and, for me, it was the first stage in my recovery after a pretty vicious mugging. The incident took place on 14 February 2016, when I was walking through a part of Cape Town I should never have been in, on my way back from watching England lose to South Africa at Newlands Cricket Ground. During the attack I was knifed, punched and kicked. With two stab wounds to my leg (not great for a runner!) and a couple of ribs kicked in, I was abandoned on a deserted street, where I lost a lot of blood. I thought my time was up. Fortunately, I was picked up and rescued.

The experience itself was awful but probably even worse when I digested what had happened once I got home. Horrid images. Horrid thoughts. It all led to a panic attack, the only one I have ever had. I tried to resolve it in the only way I could: the next morning, with two stab wounds in my left leg and a couple of broken ribs on my right-hand side, I went for a run. It was midway between Quasimodo and a duck. It hurt like hell. But it was the first time I felt the nonsense start to lift.

So yes, running is therapy. More than a year later, I am still fairly traumatised by it all and certainly can't even start to think about marathon number 31, but running is the friend who never lets you down. I'd never needed it more than in my moment of crisis – I look back on that first run as the start of the healing process.

Phil Hewitt, veteran of 30 marathons including London, Paris, Rome, Berlin, Amsterdam, Dublin, Mallorca, New York, Tokyo, La Rochelle and Marrakech – and author of Keep on Running *(Summersdale, 2012), the story of his running exploits around the world.*

Things We Hate About Running: Office Wags

When you get in from a lunchtime run, the one thing you are really hoping for is a colleague to make some side-splitting observation about your sweaty red face. Not.

Running Myths Reconsidered:
You Don't Need to do Any
Strength Training

In fact, if you are going to tackle longer distances then strength training is important. It will help enhance stability and balance, as well as keeping your muscles and joints robust.

Did you Know?

Nine billion – the number of pores per square inch in GORE-TEX fabric.

Runners You Know:
The Big Finisher (aka the kicker)

You trot around most of the course in an entirely nondescript way. Nobody even notices you ... until the final half-kilometre. Then you tighten your mouth, pump your legs and arms, and absolutely sprint the final 200 metres (200 yards) at heart-attack pace. You want a PB, after all, and besides ... you never know who might be watching.

Keep going! Keep going! (That's what she said!)

Funny Spectator Signs at Running Events

Things We Hate About Running:
Men Who Just Won't be Beaten
by a Woman

There seems to be at least one of these at every event. They run round at a steady pace, scarcely noticing if another man overtakes them, but the moment a woman passes them, they put their foot down and huff and puff their way past the 'offending' woman. Dearie me.

Running Philosophy

❝ Dancing and running shake the chemistry of happiness. **❞**

Matthew Cooley, aphorist

Remember...

Shop for running shoes late in the day, so your feet have swollen, as they will whenever you run.

Running Myths Reconsidered:
No Pain, No Gain

The philosophy that running hard is the only way to run is one that we could do without. This faux-macho nonsense, often propagated by adult-sized public schoolboys, brings little to the party. In fact, the only things it does bring are injuries, exhaustion and dismayed retirement from the hobby. If you want to go all macho on us then do it quietly. Stop trying to inflict your viewpoint on everyone else.

Running Glossary

Anaerobic threshold – this is the point during your run when lactic acid builds up in your bloodstream faster than your body can flush it out. How will you know this is happening? You'll start breathing more intensely and feel genuinely exhausted. It is also sometimes referred to as your 'lactate threshold.'

Angry resolve – the process of channelling anger over a disappointing run into your pain threshold for your next run.

Barging – when the going gets crowded at running events, some elbow-wielding bore will start forcing his way through the crowd. (It's always a 'he'.)

Carb-loading – this is the practice of chowing down large quantities of carbohydrate – pasta, bread, rice or potatoes – to boost carbohydrate reserves in your muscles. Many marathon runners carb-load in the days leading up to an event in order to maximise their fuel stores.

It's important to get this one right. On the American sitcom *The Office*, Michael Scott tucks into a huge serving of creamy *fettucine al fredo* minutes before a charity run. 'Time to carbo-load,' he says. Later, reflecting on how he went through hell during the 5k run, he says: 'I puked my guts out, but I never puked my heart out.'

Digestive issues – 'Don't trust a fart after mile 20'. There is a good reason for this sign, which I spotted at the 2016 Dublin marathon. Enough said.

Electrolytes – the things in your bodily fluids that power your muscular and brain activity. Particularly important to running are sodium and potassium.

Fartlek – Swedish for 'speed play', the fartlek is an unstructured outing in which short, fast bursts alternate with longer periods of easier running. A typical fartlek session would see a runner start with a period of warm-up, before running at full pelt towards an upcoming landmark (a lamp post or post box), then recovering before another short sprint.

The fartlek puts pressure on your aerobic and anaerobic systems, so it is a great way of building your stamina and speed. It can also mark you out as something of a spectacle. To any non-runners watching, it might appear that you are attempting, and failing, to maintain a fast burst. It's also got a funny name.

Gluteus maximus – also known simply as the 'glute', this is the most powerful muscle in the human body, and is located in the buttocks. In a technical sense, they help you extend your leg behind the body. In a vanity sense, they are the muscles that give you a perkier posterior.

Guilt – the feeling that some runners get when they spend hour after hour away from their families. This particularly affects parents of young children. However, parenting experts point out that running will make you healthier and happier, and therefore a better parent. The feeling of freedom and peace you enjoy on a run is a perfect antidote to the demanding atmosphere in the house when you've got a baby or toddler.

Hydration – all that sweating you do during the run can leave you dehydrated faster than you think. So keep your fluid levels continually topped up before, during and after your training or running event. This is one of the simple practices that runners sometimes overlook, to their detriment.

Ice cream – running 4 kilometres (2½ miles) extra and you can justify a bowl of this, guilt-free. Ah, the joys of running.

Jogger's nipple – an issue that particularly affects long-distance runners, this is a soreness of the nipple due to the incessant chafing that takes place over a marathon or other epic event.

Stand at the side of any such run and you will be able to quickly identify those who have jogger's nipple...

The problem can be avoided by applying petroleum jelly to the nipples before running. Alternatively, you can put a sticking plaster over each nipple before you set out, though the latter will set you up for a moment of pain as you later tear them off.

Kicking on – when you find that hidden energy late in a race and you are able to put your foot down. It's a wonderful feeling to kick on.

Ligament – the connective tissue that attaches bone to bone or cartilage to bone. Try not to tear it, you'll regret it if you do.

Marathons – the 26.2-miler is the most discussed of all running events. But remember, other distances are available.

Newcomer – they stand sheepishly on the sidelines at parkrun and other events, not sure whether they will ever belong. Be nice to them.

Ouch! – if you haven't barked out this word during your running life then you're not trying hard enough.

PB – personal best. Newcomers to a running event might be confused to hear hardier harriers obsessively discussing their 'PB'. Yet within no time at all, they too find themselves dreaming of that seemingly elusive gift – a new 'PB'.

Queues – they form at loos, massage tables and in front of parkrun barcode scanners. Be patient!

Rewards – medals, a fitter body, a natural high – the manifold rewards of running could fill a book. Remember them.

Shorts – with their wicking material, cutaway sides and hidden key pockets, shorts are an increasingly good friend to runners. Where would we be without them? Half naked and in the back of a police car, probably.

Space blanket – these huge, thin sheets of foil are sometimes handed to runners at the end of a long-distance race such as a marathon to keep participants warm.

Stitch – the ghastly ache in the side that can occur while running. It is usually caused by not allowing sufficient time between eating and training or not warming up correctly. There are two ways to beat it: stop running and touch your toes, or apply pressure on the area. Use your fingers to press firmly on the painful zone.

Toe nails – runners often want to shed pounds but they sometimes also lose a toe nail or two. The first sign something is wrong is when the nail starts to blacken, or it might become very painful as pressure from a bruise underneath it builds up. It then begins to loosen, before often coming off completely. Ugly. You can disguise it as a woman by painting varnish on once a thin layer of new nail has started to form.

Updates – if you get tired of running, ask yourself: am I bored of running or bored of how I am running? Try a new route for your morning run. Drive to a different parkrun. Join (or leave) your local running club. Leave your headphones at home, or take some out with you for the first time. Update your experience.

Volunteers – the quiet angels who make every running event – from parkrun to ultramarathons – go smoothly. With their luminous tabards and air of service, they are as much a mainstay of such events as the runners themselves. Give them a 'thank you'.

Water stations – a quick 'Thanks', even delivered breathlessly, never goes amiss as you take your drink from the hard-working volunteers who man these.

Xerotic – this word means 'abnormal dryness'. If you don't hydrate properly, you may begin to feel xerotic. Either way, you may feel I struggled to find a word for this letter.

Yellow jackets – have you ever volunteered at a running event? Do it. It's worth it just for the feeling of authority you feel when you don the hi-vis jacket.

Zip wire – some days, you are so tired you feel like you are running through syrup. Other days, a run is so effortless that you feel like you are on a zip wire.

Acknowledgements

First, I'd like to thank the publishing guru Lucian Randall. You've guided and supported my authorial venture in so many ways, most recently by encouraging me to write a book about running. This is that book! You're a valued friend and a ridiculously nice man. Richmond awaits us.

Thanks to the team at Bloomsbury, especially Matt Lowing. You spotted a spark and helped me fan it into a blaze. May all authors and publishing houses find an editor as attentive, enthusiastic and wise as you.

I'm grateful to Paul Davies, Jonny Cooper and Vicki Harper at the *Daily Telegraph*, for publishing so many articles from me about running.

Thanks to all my guest contributors: Liz Yelling, David Baddiel, Alastair Campbell, Nicky Campbell, Mark Watson, Ruth Field, Amy Alward, Russell Taylor, Phil Hewitt, Lisa Jackson, Paul Sinton-Hewitt, Phil Clarke, Indi Bola, Jenny Baker and Paul Tonkinson. I loved reading and sharing your stories. And to Charlotte Hardman for the crucial encouragement.

Thanks to Rob Albery for the Parkrun lifts, humour and kindness. And to the Vegan Runners, for being the best running club on the planet.

Thanks particularly to Chris for guiding and cheering me on in my writing, my running and my life. I'm not sure any words would do justice to my gratitude. You're my champion!

About The Author

Chas Newkey-Burden is a keen runner who has completed over 100 events in several countries including marathons, half-marathons and Parkruns.

He writes for dozens of publications, including the *Guardian*, *FourFourTwo*, *Shortlist* and *Attitude*. He is also the author of several books.

Follow him on Twitter: @AllThatChas

Runners You Know: The Author

You absolute moron, you're so busy people watching everyone else and trying to think of funny things to write about them, it's no wonder that you'll never improve your 5k personal best (which, incidentally, is 21:22 at the time of writing).